Mastering Financial Services:
A Comprehensive Guide to Achieving Financial Success

By T. S. Langford

Contents

INTRODUCTION

Welcome to "Mastering Financial Services: A Comprehensive Guide to Achieving Financial Success." This book was created with one goal in mind: to help you understand money, financial systems, and the services that shape your financial future. Whether you are opening your first bank account, paying off debt, building your credit, investing for retirement, or learning how to protect your assets, The financial services industry play a role in nearly every major life decision. Yet for many people, finance feels overwhelming, confusing, and even intimidating. Complex terms, endless options, and inconsistent advice can make it difficult to know where to begin. This guide is designed to replace confusion with clarity and to help you approach financial decisions with confidence.

Financial success is not reserved for the wealthy, the highly educated, or the lucky. It is built through knowledge, planning, discipline, and the ability to make informed choices. People often believe that earning more money is the only path to stability, but income alone does not guarantee financial security. Many individuals with high incomes still struggle due to overspending, poor planning, or unmanaged debt. At the same time, many people with modest incomes achieve long-term stability because they develop strong financial habits and use financial tools wisely. The difference often comes down to financial literacy. This book exists to help you develop that literacy and apply it in a practical way.

Unveiling the Blueprint for Financial Mastery

In today's world, the financial services industry is woven into everyday life more deeply than ever before. Banking, credit cards, insurance, mortgages, investments, and retirement accounts are not just optional resources—they are essential systems that influence how people live, work, and plan for the future. The financial services industry determines how easily you can buy a home, finance an education, start a business, or survive an unexpected emergency. They shape your opportunities, your level of security, and even your ability to create generational wealth.

Understanding the financial services industry is not just about knowing definitions or memorizing terminology. It is about understanding how financial systems operate and how to make them work for you. Many people fall into financial stress not because they are careless, but because they were never taught how credit works, how interest accumulates, how to budget effectively, or how to plan for retirement. Some are misled by financial myths, while others are overwhelmed by fear of making mistakes. This book is meant to break down those barriers by offering clear explanations and realistic strategies that fit modern life.

Financial mastery also requires recognizing that money is not only logical—it is emotional. People spend money based on stress, excitement, insecurity, or the desire to keep up with others. Some avoid checking their bank accounts because it triggers anxiety.

Others rely on credit cards as a safety net without fully understanding the long-term cost. Financial behavior is deeply connected to personal experiences and habits. This book does not ignore that reality. Instead, it addresses finance as both a practical skill and a personal journey, helping you build not only stronger financial strategies but also healthier financial decision-making patterns.

Why the financial services industry Matter More Than Ever

The financial world is constantly changing. Technology has transformed how people manage money. Digital banking, mobile payment systems, online investing platforms, and Cryptocurrency have expanded financial access, but they have also introduced new risks. Fraud, identity theft, and misinformation are growing concerns. In addition, economic shifts such as inflation, rising housing costs, changing job markets, and global instability have made financial planning more important than ever. Many people now face financial pressure not because they lack effort, but because the economic landscape has become more demanding and unpredictable.

Because of these changes, financial literacy is no longer optional—it is a form of self-protection. The more you understand financial services, the more power you have to make decisions that support stability and growth. When you know how loans work, you can avoid predatory lending. When you understand investing, you can build long-term wealth instead of relying solely on savings. When you learn how insurance protects your assets, you can reduce the financial damage caused by emergencies. This book will help you develop those skills in a way that is accessible and useful.

What to Expect

Each chapter in this guide is designed to build on the last, creating a structured path toward financial confidence. You will begin by exploring the basics, such as the concept of money, the role of financial institutions, and the foundations of budgeting and saving. These topics are essential because they form the backbone of personal finance. Without understanding these fundamentals, more advanced concepts like investing and wealth management can feel impossible to grasp.

As you progress, the book expands into more complex areas of financial services. You will learn about credit and debt management, including how credit scores are calculated, how interest rates affect borrowing, and how to escape cycles of high-interest debt. You will explore financial planning strategies that help you set goals, track progress, and stay motivated. You will also examine the importance of emergency funds and how to prepare for unexpected expenses without falling into financial crisis.

Investment strategies are another key focus. Many people believe investing is only for wealthy individuals, but investing is one of the most powerful tools for long-term financial growth. This book will introduce you to investment options such as stocks, bonds, mutual funds, ETFs, and retirement accounts, explaining how they work and what risks they involve. You will learn how diversification reduces risk, why time matters in investing and how compounding can grow wealth over decades. These concepts are not presented as abstract theories, but as practical tools you can apply based on your own goals and risk tolerance.

Insurance and risk management will also be explored in detail. Insurance is often overlooked until something goes wrong, yet it is one of the most important the financial services industry available. Understanding health insurance, life insurance, disability coverage, auto insurance, and property insurance can protect you from financial devastation. You will learn how to evaluate coverage options, avoid common mistakes, and choose policies that match your lifestyle.

In addition, this book will examine the regulatory landscape of financial services. Many consumers do not realize how much government regulation impacts banking, lending, and investing. Understanding regulations can help you recognize your rights, protect yourself from fraud, and make informed decisions when dealing with financial institutions. The financial services industry is not just personal—they are part of a larger system that affects economies and communities. This book will help you see how your financial decisions connect to broader economic realities.

Each chapter includes practical advice and actionable steps. The goal is not only to teach you concepts, but to help you apply them in real life. Financial knowledge is only valuable when it changes behavior and leads to better decision-making. For that reason, this guide focuses heavily on strategies you can implement immediately, whether that means creating a budget, improving your credit score, building an emergency fund, or developing a long-term investment plan.

Your Path to Financial Empowerment Starts Here

Financial empowerment means having control over your choices. It means being able to make decisions based on knowledge rather than fear. It means understanding what options exist and knowing how to use them to build stability and freedom. Financial empowerment does not require perfection. Mistakes are common, and setbacks happen to everyone. What matters is learning how to recover, adapt, and continue moving forward with intention.

This book is designed to meet you where you are. If you are just starting your financial journey, it will provide you with a strong foundation and guidance for building smart habits. If you are already financially experienced, it will offer deeper insight into wealth-building strategies and advanced financial planning. If you are recovering from financial hardship, it will provide tools to rebuild and regain confidence. No matter your background, the goal is the same: to help you develop the knowledge and skills necessary to create a future that is financially stable and personally meaningful.

This journey is about more than numbers. It is about security, independence, and opportunity. It is about being prepared for emergencies instead of being destroyed by them. It is about building a life where money supports your goals rather than controlling your choices. Whether you dream of homeownership, retirement freedom, entrepreneurship, travel, or simply living without constant financial stress, the strategies in this book can help you get there.

As you move forward, remember that financial success is not achieved overnight. It is built through steady progress, consistent effort, and the willingness to learn. The most important step is the decision to begin. With the right knowledge and tools, you can take control of your financial life, make informed decisions, and create a future defined by stability, growth, and confidence. Welcome to your journey toward mastering financial services.

THE FOUNDATIONS OF FINANCIAL SERVICES

A deeper understanding of the foundations of the financial services industry requires recognizing that money is not only a practical tool but also a powerful force that shapes decision-making, opportunity, and long-term stability. Money influences nearly every aspect of modern life, from basic survival needs to future ambitions. The financial services industry exists to help individuals and businesses manage money more effectively, providing structure, safety, and strategies for growth. By understanding the fundamental building blocks of financial systems, you begin to see how personal finances connect to the larger economy and how everyday decisions can have lasting consequences.

The Concept of Money

Money is often described as the lifeblood of the economy because it allows societies to exchange goods and services efficiently. Before money existed, people relied on barter systems, trading one item directly for another. While barter could work in small communities, it created major limitations. For example, if one person had grain and wanted shoes, they needed to find someone who both had shoes and wanted grain. This "double coincidence of wants" made trade slow and unreliable. Money solved this problem by acting as a universal medium of exchange.

Over time, money evolved from physical commodities like salt, cattle, and precious metals into coins, paper currency, and now digital transactions. Modern money is no longer tied to gold or physical reserves in most countries. Instead, it is considered "fiat money," meaning it has value because governments declare it valuable and people trust the system behind it. This trust is essential. Currency only works when people believe it can be exchanged for goods and services tomorrow just as it can today.

Money serves three main functions: it is a medium of exchange, a unit of account, and a store of value. As a medium of exchange, it allows transactions to happen smoothly. As a unit of account, it provides a consistent way to measure value, making it easier to compare prices and calculate costs. As a store of value, it allows individuals to save purchasing power for the future. This third function is closely tied to inflation, which occurs when prices rise and money buys less over time. Inflation reduces purchasing power, which is why saving money without earning interest or investing can weaken financial stability in the long run.

Understanding inflation also introduces an important idea: time affects money. A dollar today is not worth the same as a dollar ten years from now because its purchasing power changes. This is why interest rates matter. Interest is essentially the cost of borrowing money or the reward for saving it. When you borrow money, you pay interest because the lender is giving you purchasing power today. When you save or invest money, you earn interest or returns because you are delaying your use of money and taking on some level of risk.

Money is also deeply connected to behavior. People do not always make rational financial choices, even when they know what the "best" option is. Emotional spending, fear of missing out, and financial anxiety often influence decisions. Learning about money means learning about yourself as well—your habits, priorities, and vulnerabilities. Financial literacy is not only about math; it is about building awareness and discipline.

The Role of Financial Institutions

Financial institutions play a central role in keeping money flowing through the economy. These institutions include banks, credit unions, investment firms, insurance companies, pension funds, and financial technology companies. Their purpose is to provide services that allow individuals and businesses to store money safely, access credit, transfer funds, manage risk, and build wealth.

Banks and credit unions are the most familiar financial institutions. They accept deposits and provide accounts such as checking and savings accounts. Deposits serve two purposes. For consumers, deposits provide security and easy access to money. For banks, deposits provide the funds needed to lend money to others. When banks lend money, they charge interest, which becomes a major source of profit. This system is often described as financial intermediation—banks act as the middle layer between savers and borrowers.

Loans are one of the most significant services offered by financial institutions. People borrow money to purchase homes, pay for education, start businesses, or manage emergencies. Loans can be secured or unsecured. Secured loans are backed by collateral, such as a house or car, which reduces the lender's risk. Mortgages and auto loans are examples of secured loans. Unsecured loans, such as credit cards and personal loans, do not have collateral, so lenders charge higher interest rates to compensate for the risk.

Financial institutions also provide credit, which is closely tied to a person's credit score and credit history. Credit scores are numerical ratings that estimate how likely someone is to repay borrowed money. A strong credit score can lead to lower interest rates and easier access to loans, while a weak credit score can create financial barriers. Credit is not automatically harmful—it can be a powerful tool when managed wisely. The danger comes when people borrow beyond their means, rely on credit for daily expenses, or fall into cycles of high-interest debt.

Beyond traditional banking, investment firms and brokerage institutions allow individuals to participate in wealth-building opportunities. Investments include stocks, bonds, mutual funds, exchange-traded funds (ETFs), and retirement accounts. These tools help individuals grow their wealth over time, but they also carry varying degrees of risk. The relationship between risk and reward is a key principle in financial services:

generally, the greater the potential return, the higher the potential risk.

Insurance companies also play an essential role in financial stability. Insurance is designed to protect individuals from financial loss. Health insurance, life insurance, disability insurance, car insurance, and home insurance all serve as forms of risk management. Instead of facing a catastrophic financial burden alone, individuals pay regular premiums so the insurance company can cover major losses when they occur. This reduces uncertainty and protects long-term financial security.

In recent years, financial technology has expanded rapidly. Online banking, mobile apps, digital wallets, and automated investing platforms have made the financial services industry more accessible than ever. These innovations provide convenience and efficiency, but they also create new concerns about data privacy, cybersecurity, and fraud. The ability to access financial accounts instantly can be empowering, but it can also encourage impulsive decisions. Technology has improved financial services, but it has also increased the need for strong financial awareness and responsibility.

Building a Solid Financial Foundation

A strong financial foundation is built on habits, planning, and self-control. Many people assume financial success is determined by income alone, but income is only one piece of the puzzle. What matters most is how money is managed. Someone with a high income can still struggle financially if spending is uncontrolled, debt is unmanaged, or saving is neglected. On the other hand, someone with a modest income can build long-term stability through disciplined habits and smart planning.

Budgeting is one of the most basic and effective tools for financial management. A budget is a plan that tracks income and expenses, allowing individuals to understand where their money goes. Budgeting helps identify wasteful spending, encourages intentional decision-making, and supports financial goals. Without a budget, many people rely on guesswork, which often leads to overspending and financial stress.

Saving is another critical pillar of financial stability. Saving provides protection and flexibility. Emergency savings are especially important because unexpected expenses are a normal part of life. Car repairs, medical costs, job loss, or family emergencies can quickly create financial chaos if there is no savings buffer. A common recommendation is to save three to six months' worth of living expenses, though the ideal amount varies depending on income stability and personal circumstances.

Managing debt is equally important. Debt is not always harmful, but it must be handled carefully. Some forms of debt, such as mortgages or student loans, may support long-term growth and opportunity. High-interest consumer debt, such as credit card balances, is often more damaging because interest charges can accumulate rapidly. Debt becomes dangerous when it prevents saving, reduces financial freedom, and creates long-term stress. Paying down high-interest debt is often one of the most effective steps toward financial stability.

Building financial strength also requires understanding interest and compounding. Compound interest allows money to grow faster over time because interest is earned not only on the original amount but also on accumulated interest. This concept applies to savings and investments, but it also applies to debt. Credit card debt grows through compound interest in the opposite direction, becoming more expensive the longer it remains unpaid. Learning how compounding works is one of the most powerful financial lessons because it highlights the importance of starting early and staying consistent.

In addition to budgeting and saving, investing is often necessary for long-term goals. Many people assume saving alone is enough, but inflation reduces purchasing power, meaning money that sits idle may lose value over time. Investing allows individuals to grow their wealth and stay ahead of inflation. Retirement planning is one of the clearest examples of why investing matters. Pension plans and government benefits may not be sufficient for comfortable retirement, so personal retirement accounts and long-term investments become essential.

Another key part of building a financial foundation is goal setting. Financial goals give direction and motivation. Goals may include paying off debt, saving for a home, building an emergency fund, or investing for retirement. Breaking large goals into smaller steps makes them more achievable and helps individuals stay consistent. Financial success is rarely the result of one major decision; it is more often the result of repeated small decisions made over time.

The Regulatory Landscape

The financial services industry operates within a complex regulatory environment designed to protect consumers, prevent fraud, and maintain economic stability. Without regulation, financial institutions could exploit consumers more easily, engage in reckless practices, or create instability that affects the entire economy. Financial regulations exist to ensure fairness, transparency, and accountability.

Regulatory bodies vary by country, but their responsibilities often include monitoring banks, enforcing lending standards, protecting depositors, and overseeing investment markets. These agencies ensure that financial institutions hold enough reserves to remain stable, follow ethical practices, and provide accurate information to consumers. Regulations also help prevent money laundering, identity theft, and illegal financial activity.

One of the most important consumer protections is transparency in lending. Many regulations require lenders to clearly disclose interest rates, repayment terms, fees, and penalties. This is crucial because borrowing agreements can be complex, and consumers may not always understand what they are signing. When borrowers understand the true cost of loans, they can make more informed choices and avoid being trapped in predatory lending situations.

Deposit insurance is another major regulatory feature that provides stability. Many governments insure deposits up to a certain amount, ensuring that consumers do not lose all their money if a bank fails. This system builds trust in financial institutions and reduces the risk of panic withdrawals that could destabilize the economy.

Regulations also influence investment markets. Securities regulators oversee stock exchanges, trading practices, and investment disclosures. These regulations help reduce fraud, insider trading, and manipulation. While no system can eliminate financial risk entirely, regulation provides structure that makes markets safer and more predictable.

Financial regulations often evolve after major economic crises. When recessions or market collapses occur, governments tend to introduce stricter rules to prevent the same problems from repeating. Understanding the regulatory landscape helps consumers recognize their rights, understand how financial systems are protected, and become more confident when working with financial institutions.

Embracing Financial Literacy

Financial literacy is the ability to understand and apply financial knowledge in everyday life. It includes skills such as budgeting, saving, investing, managing debt, understanding credit, and interpreting financial products. Financial literacy is one of the strongest tools for building independence because it reduces vulnerability. People who lack financial knowledge are more likely to fall into debt traps, become victims of scams, or make decisions that harm their long-term security.

Financial literacy also builds confidence. Many people avoid financial topics because they feel overwhelmed or intimidated. However, financial concepts become easier when learned step by step. Understanding basic terms like interest rates, inflation, credit utilization, and investment risk can make a major difference in financial decision-making. When individuals develop financial knowledge, they gain the ability to evaluate options rather than relying on guesswork or emotional reactions.

Continuous learning is essential because financial systems change over time. New technologies, new investment products, and shifting economic conditions all influence financial decision-making. Reading books, taking online courses, following reputable financial news sources, and speaking with certified financial professionals can help individuals stay informed.

Financial literacy is not about becoming a financial expert—it is about building the ability to protect yourself, plan wisely, and make decisions that support stability and long-term success. By understanding the foundations of financial services, you gain insight into how money works, how institutions operate, and how financial decisions shape the future. With this knowledge, the financial services industry stops feeling confusing or intimidating and start becoming tools that can support growth, security, and personal empowerment.

UNDERSTANDING INVESTMENT STRATEGIES

In this chapter, we shift our focus to the world of investing, where careful planning and informed decision-making can turn long-term financial goals into reality. Investing is one of the most effective ways to build wealth over time, but it also comes with risks that require thoughtful management. Whether you are investing for retirement, building savings for future milestones, or seeking financial independence, understanding investment strategies gives you the tools to grow your money with purpose. The investment world can seem complex at first, filled with unfamiliar terminology and endless choices, but the core principles remain consistent: balance risk, remain disciplined, and make decisions based on strategy rather than emotion.

Investing is not simply about picking the "right" stock or finding a quick opportunity. Strong investing is built on structure. It involves understanding your personal goals, determining your timeline, and choosing investment options that align with your risk tolerance. A well-developed strategy can help you avoid costly mistakes, such as chasing trends, panic-selling during market declines, or placing too much of your money into one area. When investing is approached with patience and knowledge, it becomes a long-term system for creating stability and financial growth.

Diversification and Risk Management

Diversification is one of the most important concepts in investing because it protects your portfolio from being overly dependent on one investment or one market sector. Diversification means spreading your money across different types of investments, such as stocks, bonds, real estate, and cash equivalents. It can also mean spreading investments across different industries, geographic regions, and company sizes. The goal is to reduce the damage that any single poor-performing investment can cause.

If all your money is placed into one stock and that company performs badly, your portfolio could lose significant value. If your money is spread across many assets, losses in one area may be offset by gains or stability in another. Diversification does not eliminate risk entirely, but it reduces the impact of volatility and helps smooth out long-term performance. This is why diversified portfolios are often considered more resilient, especially during uncertain economic periods.

Risk management also includes understanding your own comfort level with uncertainty. Some investors can tolerate large swings in portfolio value, while others become anxious when markets decline. A strategy that matches your risk tolerance is more likely to be sustainable, because it reduces the chances of emotional decision-making. Risk management is not about avoiding risk completely—it is about taking the right kind of risk for your goals and timeline.

Investment Vehicles: Stocks and Bonds

Stocks and bonds are two of the most common investment vehicles and are often considered the foundation of most portfolios. Stocks represent ownership in a company. When you buy stock, you become a shareholder, meaning you own a small portion of that business. Stocks can generate returns in two main ways: through capital appreciation, which occurs when the stock price rises, and through dividends, which are payments made to shareholders from company profits.

Stocks are often associated with higher potential returns, but they also come with higher volatility. Stock prices can rise or fall quickly due to company performance, economic conditions, industry trends, or global events. Over the long term, stocks have historically been one of the strongest wealth-building tools, but they require patience and the ability to tolerate market fluctuations.

Bonds, on the other hand, function more like loans. When you buy a bond, you are lending money to a government or corporation in exchange for regular interest payments and the return of your original investment at maturity. Bonds are typically seen as lower-risk investments compared to stocks, although they still carry risks such as interest rate changes and issuer default. Bonds can provide steady income and stability, making them valuable for investors who want to reduce volatility in their portfolios.

Understanding the relationship between stocks and bonds is essential because they often respond differently to market conditions. Many investors use bonds to balance out stock exposure, especially when approaching retirement or other major financial milestones.

Exploring Alternative Investments

Alternative investments are assets that fall outside traditional categories like stocks and bonds. These can include real estate, commodities (such as gold or oil), hedge funds, private equity, collectibles, and even newer options like Cryptocurrency . Alternative investments are often used to further diversify a portfolio, since they may not move in the same direction as traditional markets.

Real estate is one of the most common alternative investments. It can provide long-term growth through property value appreciation and also generate income through rental payments. Real estate can be appealing because it is tangible and often considered a hedge against inflation. However, it also comes with challenges such as property maintenance, market downturns, and liquidity issues, since selling property takes time.

Commodities like gold and oil can act as a hedge against inflation or economic uncertainty, but they can also be unpredictable and heavily influenced by global events. Cryptocurrency has attracted many investors due to its high growth potential, but it remains extremely volatile and carries significant regulatory and security concerns.

Alternative investments can strengthen a portfolio when used strategically, but they also require careful research. Many alternative assets are less regulated, harder to value, and less liquid than traditional investments. They can provide opportunity, but they demand a higher level of awareness and caution.

Understanding Investment Risks

Every investment carries risk, and understanding risk is essential to developing a resilient strategy. Market risk refers to the possibility that an investment will lose value due to overall market declines. Even strong companies can experience stock drops during recessions or major economic disruptions. Liquidity risk refers to the difficulty of selling an investment quickly without losing value. Real estate and collectibles are examples of assets that can be difficult to liquidate.

Interest rate risk is especially important for bond investors. When interest rates rise, existing bonds often lose value because newer bonds offer better returns. Inflation risk is another major concern, as inflation reduces the purchasing power of money over time. If investment returns fail to outpace inflation, your wealth may lose real value even if the numbers in your account grow.

Geopolitical risk includes instability caused by wars, political conflict, global trade disruptions, or international crises. These events can influence markets quickly and unexpectedly. Understanding these categories of risk allows investors to prepare, rather than react in panic when markets become unstable. A strong investment strategy accepts that risk is unavoidable, but it focuses on managing risk intelligently.

The Role of Financial Advisors

Financial advisors can play a valuable role in helping individuals navigate investments, especially when goals become complex or large amounts of money are involved. Advisors may help with retirement planning, investment selection, tax strategies, insurance planning, and long-term wealth management. For many investors, professional guidance provides clarity and structure, reducing uncertainty and preventing costly mistakes.

Choosing the right advisor is critical. Investors should seek professionals with recognized credentials, transparency, and a clear explanation of how they are paid. Some advisors earn commissions from products they sell, while others charge flat fees or a percentage of assets under management. Understanding this compensation structure is important because it can influence the advice you receive.

A strong advisor-client relationship should be based on trust, communication, and alignment. An advisor should not push investments that do not match your risk tolerance or financial goals. Their job is not to take control of your finances, but to guide you, educate you, and support your decision-making process.

Asset Allocation Strategies

Asset allocation refers to how your investments are divided among different asset classes, such as stocks, bonds, cash, and alternative investments. It is one of the most important factors influencing long-term portfolio performance. Asset allocation is based on your timeline, goals, and risk tolerance. For example, younger investors often allocate more toward stocks because they have time to recover from market downturns. Older investors nearing retirement often allocate more toward bonds and stable investments to reduce volatility.

Asset allocation is not a one-time decision. Over time, some investments may grow faster than others, causing your portfolio to drift away from your original balance. This is where rebalancing becomes essential. Rebalancing means adjusting your portfolio back to its intended allocation by selling some assets and buying others. This keeps risk levels consistent and prevents your portfolio from becoming too heavily weighted in one area.

A well-designed asset allocation strategy creates structure and discipline. It helps investors avoid emotional investing and keeps their portfolio aligned with their long-term plan.

Market Analysis and Research

Successful investing requires research and an understanding of how markets function. Fundamental analysis focuses on evaluating the financial health of a company by reviewing revenue, profit, debt levels, competitive position, and long-term growth potential. Investors using fundamental analysis look at whether a company is undervalued or overvalued based on its performance and potential.

Technical analysis takes a different approach by studying price patterns, trading volume, and market trends. This method is often used by traders seeking short-term opportunities, though long-term investors may also use technical signals to help time entry points.

Market research also involves paying attention to economic indicators such as inflation rates, employment reports, interest rate changes, and consumer confidence. Global events and political decisions can also influence markets, sometimes rapidly. While no one can predict the market perfectly, staying informed helps investors make decisions based on evidence rather than speculation.

Tax-Efficient Investing

Taxes can significantly reduce investment returns if they are not managed carefully. Tax-efficient investing involves strategies that reduce the amount of taxes paid on gains, dividends, and interest. One common approach is using tax-advantaged accounts, such as retirement accounts that allow tax-deferred growth or tax-free withdrawals depending on the account type.

Another strategy is investing in tax-efficient funds, which are designed to minimize taxable distributions. Capital gains harvesting and tax-loss harvesting are also valuable tools. Tax-loss harvesting involves selling investments at a loss to offset gains in other areas, reducing taxable income. These strategies require planning and awareness, but they can improve after-tax returns and strengthen long-term results.

Tax efficiency is often overlooked, but it can make a major difference over decades of investing. Smart investing is not only about what you earn—it is also about what you keep.

Behavioral Finance

Behavioral finance examines how psychology affects investing decisions. Many investors believe they are rational, but emotions often drive decisions more than logic. Fear can lead to panic-selling during market downturns, while greed can lead to reckless investing during market booms. Overconfidence may cause investors to take unnecessary risks, while loss aversion can cause them to hold onto failing investments for too long.

Common biases include confirmation bias, where investors seek information that supports their beliefs, and herd mentality, where investors follow trends because others are doing so. These behaviors can lead to buying high and selling low, which is the opposite of what successful investing requires.

Understanding behavioral finance helps investors recognize emotional triggers and build strategies to protect themselves from impulsive decisions. Discipline, consistency, and long-term thinking are often more powerful than trying to outsmart the market.

Continuous Learning and Adaptation

The investment world is constantly evolving. New financial products, market trends, and global developments can reshape the landscape quickly. Successful investors commit to continuous learning, staying informed about economic changes, industry innovations, and financial tools. Learning does not mean constantly changing your strategy, but it does mean staying aware of how external conditions might affect your portfolio.

Adaptation is also essential. As your life changes—through career growth, family responsibilities, homeownership, or retirement planning—your investment strategy should evolve as well. A portfolio that worked in your twenties may not be appropriate in your fifties. Adjusting asset allocation, risk exposure, and long-term goals ensures your investments remain aligned with your reality.

Investing is not a one-time event. It is an ongoing process built on patience, planning, and discipline. With the right strategies, investing becomes a powerful tool for building wealth, protecting financial security, and creating a future where your money supports your life goals rather than limiting them.

NAVIGATING THE WORLD OF BANKING

Banking is one of the most essential pillars of financial services, shaping how individuals and businesses manage, store, borrow, and grow money. Nearly every financial journey begins with a bank account, making banking one of the first and most influential financial relationships a person develops. While banks are often seen as simple places to deposit money and withdraw cash, the modern banking system is far more complex. It provides services that support daily transactions, long-term savings, credit access, wealth-building, and economic stability. Understanding how banking works empowers you to use these services strategically rather than passively, helping you protect your money, reduce financial stress, and create opportunities for growth.

Banking has also undergone dramatic transformation in recent decades. Traditional in-person banking is now supported and often replaced by digital services that allow consumers to manage finances instantly. With this evolution comes both convenience and risk. Navigating the banking world effectively means understanding the core services banks provide, recognizing how credit and interest work, learning how to protect yourself from fraud, and staying informed about innovations that may influence your financial future.

Core Banking Services

At the heart of banking are the core services that help people manage their everyday finances. The most common banking products include checking accounts, savings accounts, and certificates of deposit (CDs). Each serves a different purpose, and understanding their roles allows you to make smarter financial decisions.

A checking account is designed for frequent transactions. It is commonly used for receiving paychecks, paying bills, withdrawing cash, and making purchases through debit cards. Checking accounts provide easy access to money, but they typically offer low or no interest. Because of this, checking accounts are best used for managing monthly expenses rather than long-term savings. Many banks offer features such as overdraft protection, bill payment systems, and automatic transfers, all of which can improve financial organization when used wisely.

Savings accounts are intended for storing money over time while earning interest. They are ideal for emergency funds, short-term goals, and saving for planned purchases. While savings account interest rates are often modest, they provide a safer option than keeping cash at home. Savings accounts also encourage disciplined financial habits, especially when paired with automatic deposits.

Certificates of deposit offer a more structured savings option. When you open a CD, you agree to leave your money in the account for a fixed period of time in exchange for a higher interest rate. CDs are useful for individuals who want guaranteed returns and do not need immediate access to their funds. However, early withdrawal penalties can apply, so CDs work best for planned savings goals with clear timelines.

By understanding these basic banking products, you can create a system where your money is organized with intention: checking for spending, savings for security, and CDs for longer-term stability.

Digital Banking and the FinTech Revolution

The rise of digital banking has reshaped the financial services industry in ways that were unimaginable just a few decades ago. Online banking platforms and mobile apps allow individuals to check balances, transfer funds, deposit checks, and pay bills from anywhere. This convenience has made banking more accessible and efficient, reducing the need for in-person visits and giving people greater control over their finances.

Financial technology, often called FinTech, has further expanded banking options. FinTech companies offer digital-only banking services, budgeting tools, peer-to-peer payment systems, and automated investing platforms. These innovations often provide lower fees, faster transactions, and user-friendly interfaces. Services like digital wallets and instant payment systems have also made it easier for people to manage money in real time.

However, the convenience of digital banking also introduces challenges. The speed of online transactions can make overspending easier, and constant access to financial accounts may increase impulsive financial behavior. Digital banking also increases exposure to cybersecurity threats. Learning how to use these tools responsibly is essential. Digital banking should be seen as a powerful advantage, but one that requires careful attention to security and financial discipline.

Credit Facilities: Loans and Credit Cards

One of the most significant roles banks play is providing access to credit. Credit allows individuals to borrow money for major expenses, emergencies, or long-term investments such as education and homeownership. Banks offer many forms of credit, including personal loans, mortgages, auto loans, student loans, and credit cards.

Loans provide borrowers with a lump sum of money that must be repaid over time with interest. Loan terms vary depending on the type of loan, credit history, and lender policies. A key factor in loans is the interest rate, which determines the cost of borrowing. Interest rates can be fixed, meaning they remain stable, or variable, meaning they can change based on market conditions. Understanding these differences is critical because interest rates can dramatically affect monthly payments and long-term costs.

Credit cards operate differently than loans. Instead of receiving a lump sum, credit cards provide a revolving line of credit that can be used repeatedly. Credit cards can be useful tools when managed responsibly. They can help build credit history, provide rewards such as cash back, and offer consumer protections against fraud. However, credit cards also carry high interest rates, making them dangerous if balances are not paid off quickly.

Responsible credit management includes paying bills on time, keeping balances low, and avoiding unnecessary borrowing. When credit is used strategically, it can support financial growth. When misused, it can become a long-term burden that limits future opportunities.

Banking Security and Fraud Prevention

As banking becomes more digital, protecting financial information has become a major priority. Banks use a variety of security measures, including encryption, two-factor authentication, biometric identification, fraud monitoring systems, and transaction alerts. These tools are designed to detect suspicious activity and prevent unauthorized access to accounts.

Despite these protections, fraud remains a growing concern. Common threats include phishing scams, identity theft, credit card fraud, and account hacking. Phishing occurs when criminals impersonate banks or trusted organizations through emails or text messages, attempting to steal personal information such as passwords or account numbers. Identity theft involves using someone's personal information to open accounts, take loans, or commit financial crimes.

Consumers play an important role in fraud prevention. Using strong passwords, enabling security alerts, avoiding public Wi-Fi for banking transactions, and monitoring account activity regularly can significantly reduce risk. It is also important to recognize warning signs, such as unexpected account notifications or unauthorized transactions. Being proactive with banking security protects not only your money, but also your financial future.

The Evolving Role of Banks in the Global Economy

Banks are not only important to individuals—they are essential to the global economy. They facilitate economic growth by providing loans to businesses, supporting entrepreneurship, and funding major infrastructure projects. Banks also play a major role in international trade by enabling currency exchange, managing cross-border transactions, and supporting global investment flows.

The global banking system is deeply interconnected. Events in one country can influence markets and banking stability in others. Economic downturns, political instability, inflation, and global crises can all affect banking systems worldwide. Understanding this interconnectedness helps individuals recognize why interest rates change, why currencies fluctuate, and why financial markets sometimes become unstable.

Banks also influence national economies through monetary policy. Central banks, such as the Federal Reserve in the United States or the Bank of Canada, regulate money supply and interest rates to control inflation and encourage economic stability. These policies directly impact borrowing costs, mortgage rates, and investment opportunities, meaning banking decisions are tied closely to economic conditions.

Investment and Wealth Management

Many banks offer wealth management and investment services designed to help customers grow their money. These services may include mutual funds, brokerage accounts, bonds, stocks, retirement accounts, and managed portfolios. Banks often provide investment advisors who help clients choose strategies aligned with their goals, timelines, and risk tolerance.

Wealth management is especially valuable for individuals who want structured guidance. It involves not only investing, but also long-term financial planning, estate planning, and risk management. Understanding diversification and risk tolerance is essential in this area, as investing requires balancing potential returns with the possibility of loss.

Bank investment services can be convenient, but it is also important to compare fees, performance, and advisor incentives. Some products may carry higher fees than alternatives, which can reduce long-term returns. Learning how to evaluate investment offerings ensures you remain in control of your wealth-building strategy.

Retirement Planning and Pension Services

Banks also support retirement planning through savings products and investment accounts designed for long-term growth. Retirement planning often includes tools such as pension plans, retirement savings accounts, employer-sponsored programs, and long-term investment portfolios.

Retirement planning is not only about saving money, but about building a strategy that accounts for inflation, healthcare costs, and long-term living expenses. Many individuals underestimate how much money they will need in retirement, especially as life expectancy increases. Banking services can help individuals structure retirement contributions, invest for long-term growth, and create withdrawal strategies for later years.

Retirement accounts often come with tax advantages, making them powerful tools for building wealth. Understanding how these accounts work allows individuals to maximize contributions and create long-term security.

Corporate and Business Banking

Business banking is another major function of the banking industry. Banks provide the financial services industry to companies of all sizes, from small startups to multinational corporations. Business accounts allow companies to manage cash flow, process payroll, and track expenses. Banks also offer merchant services that allow businesses to accept debit and credit card payments.

Business loans are essential for expansion, equipment purchases, and operational stability. Banks may provide lines of credit, commercial loans, and financing solutions tailored to business needs. Business credit is especially important because it separates personal finances from business operations, reducing risk for entrepreneurs.

Corporate banking also includes investment services, large-scale financing, and support for international business transactions. Understanding business banking is essential for anyone interested in entrepreneurship because banking relationships often determine how easily a business can grow.

Financial Education and Literacy Programs

Many banks now provide educational resources to help customers improve financial literacy. These resources may include budgeting workshops, credit-building programs, online financial courses, and tools for tracking spending. Financial education is increasingly recognized as a key part of consumer protection because financially informed customers are less likely to fall into debt traps or financial scams.

Using these programs can strengthen your ability to manage

money effectively. Even basic financial education can improve decision-making and reduce financial stress. Banking literacy programs are valuable resources because they often provide practical, real-world guidance that applies directly to everyday finances.

Environmental, Social, and Governance (ESG) Banking

Modern banking is also shifting toward sustainability and social responsibility. ESG banking focuses on environmental impact, social responsibility, and ethical governance. Some banks now offer green investment products, sustainable lending programs, and policies that limit investments in industries considered harmful to the environment or society.

Consumers can participate in ESG banking by choosing banks and financial products that align with their values. This may include supporting institutions that invest in renewable energy, promote fair lending practices, or fund community development projects. ESG banking reflects a growing recognition that financial decisions have broader impacts beyond personal profit.

Regulatory Landscape and Consumer Rights

Banks operate under strict regulations designed to protect consumers and maintain economic stability. Regulations govern lending practices, interest rate transparency, fraud prevention, and consumer privacy. These laws help prevent abusive financial practices and ensure that banks operate responsibly.

Consumer rights include access to fair lending, clear disclosure of fees, and protection against unauthorized transactions. Understanding these rights empowers you to challenge unfair charges, avoid predatory loans, and make informed decisions when choosing banking products. Regulatory agencies exist to enforce these protections, and consumers benefit greatly from knowing how these systems work.

Emerging Trends in Banking

The future of banking is being shaped by rapid technological innovation. Artificial intelligence is being used for fraud detection, customer service chatbots, and personalized financial planning tools. Blockchain technology is creating new possibilities for secure transactions and decentralized finance. Digital currencies, including central bank digital currencies, are also being explored as potential alternatives to traditional cash systems.

Decentralized finance, known as DeFi, is another emerging trend. DeFi platforms allow individuals to lend, borrow, and invest without traditional banks acting as intermediaries. While these systems offer innovation and accessibility, they also carry high risks due to limited regulation and volatility.

Banking is evolving quickly, and staying informed about these trends helps individuals prepare for future changes. The more you understand the direction banking is heading, the better positioned you are to take advantage of new tools while avoiding unnecessary risk.

By exploring the many dimensions of banking—from core accounts and credit systems to global economics and emerging innovations—you gain a stronger understanding of how banks influence daily life and long-term financial success. Banking is not simply a place to store money. It is a powerful system that can support stability, wealth-building, and opportunity when used with knowledge, strategy, and awareness.

INSURANCE ESSENTIALS FOR FINANCIAL SECURITY

Insurance is one of the most important, yet often misunderstood, pillars of financial planning. Many people view insurance as an unnecessary expense—something they pay for but hope they never use. In reality, insurance is a powerful tool for protecting your financial stability and preventing life's unexpected events from turning into long-term financial hardship. While savings and investments help build wealth, insurance helps protect it. Without proper coverage, a single accident, illness, or disaster can wipe out years of progress and leave individuals and families struggling to recover.

Insurance works by spreading risk across many people. Policyholders pay premiums into a shared system, and when someone experiences a covered loss, the insurance company helps cover the financial cost. This system provides protection against events that would otherwise be too expensive for most individuals to handle alone. From medical emergencies to property damage, insurance offers peace of mind and financial security by acting as a safeguard against uncertainty. A comprehensive financial plan is not complete without understanding insurance, because true financial success is not only about growth—it is also about protection.

Types of Insurance Coverage

Insurance comes in many forms, each designed to protect against specific risks. Understanding the purpose of each type helps you make informed decisions about what coverage you need and what level of protection is appropriate for your life situation. Common types of insurance include life insurance, health insurance, property insurance, auto insurance, disability insurance, and liability insurance.

Life insurance protects your loved ones financially if you pass away. Health insurance protects you from the high cost of medical care. Property insurance covers damage or loss related to your home and belongings. Auto insurance provides coverage for accidents, repairs, and liability. Disability insurance replaces income if you become unable to work due to illness or injury. Liability insurance protects you if you are legally responsible for harming someone or damaging their property.

Each of these insurance types serves a different role, but together they create a safety net that supports long-term stability. The right insurance coverage depends on your income, family responsibilities, health, assets, lifestyle, and risk exposure. Insurance is not one-size-fits-all. It must be tailored to your personal needs and financial goals.

Life Insurance: Planning for the Future

Life insurance is a cornerstone of financial planning because it provides financial security for the people who depend on you. In the event of your death, life insurance can help cover funeral costs, replace lost income, pay off debts, fund children's education, and provide ongoing support for your family. Without life insurance, surviving family members may face serious financial strain, especially if they relied on your income.

Life insurance is especially important for parents, homeowners with mortgages, business owners, and individuals who support spouses or relatives. Even young adults may benefit from life insurance if they have debts or responsibilities that could become a burden for family members.

There are two main types of life insurance: term life insurance and whole life insurance. Term life insurance provides coverage for a specific period, such as 10, 20, or 30 years. It is generally more affordable and straightforward. Many people choose term insurance because it offers strong protection during the years when financial responsibilities are highest, such as raising children or paying off a mortgage. The downside is that term policies do not build cash value, and coverage ends when the term expires unless it is renewed.

Whole life insurance provides coverage for the policyholder's entire life. It includes a cash value component that grows over time, which can act as a savings feature. Whole life policies offer stable premiums and lifelong protection, but they are significantly more expensive than term insurance. Some people use whole life insurance as part of long-term wealth planning, but it is not the best fit for everyone. Choosing between term and whole life insurance depends on your financial priorities, budget, and goals. For many families, term insurance provides the strongest balance of affordability and protection.

When selecting life insurance, it is important to evaluate how much coverage you need. This is often based on income replacement, outstanding debts, future expenses, and long-term family needs. The purpose of life insurance is not simply to cover funeral expenses—it is meant to protect your family's ability to maintain stability if you are no longer there to provide support.

Health Insurance: Navigating Healthcare Costs

Health insurance is one of the most essential forms of coverage because healthcare costs can be devastating without it. A single medical emergency, hospitalization, or long-term illness can create financial burdens that last for years. Health insurance reduces these risks by covering a portion of medical expenses, helping individuals access necessary care without facing overwhelming debt.

Health insurance policies typically include several important components. Premiums are the monthly payments required to maintain coverage. Deductibles represent the amount you must pay out of pocket before insurance begins covering costs. Copayments and coinsurance are additional expenses that may apply when receiving treatment, such as visiting a doctor or filling prescriptions. Out-of-pocket maximums are also critical, as they set a limit on how much you will pay in a year before insurance covers the rest.

Most health insurance plans also include preventive care benefits, such as checkups, screenings, and vaccinations. Preventive care is valuable because it can detect health issues early and reduce long-term healthcare costs. Prescription drug coverage is another key feature, especially for individuals managing chronic conditions. Without prescription coverage, medication costs can quickly become unmanageable.

Navigating health insurance requires careful attention to details. Choosing the right plan involves evaluating your health needs, budget, and access to preferred doctors and hospitals. Understanding your policy ensures you know what is covered, what is not, and how to avoid unexpected expenses. Health insurance is not just about emergencies—it supports ongoing health maintenance and financial protection.

Property and Casualty Insurance

Property and casualty insurance protects valuable assets such as your home, car, and personal belongings.

These assets often represent years of savings and financial effort. Without insurance, damage from accidents, theft, or natural disasters could result in significant financial loss.

Homeowners insurance provides protection for your home structure and the belongings inside it. It may also cover additional living expenses if your home becomes uninhabitable due to a covered event. Homeowners insurance is essential for anyone who owns property, especially since home repairs can be extremely expensive. Coverage typically includes protection against fire, theft, vandalism, and certain weather-related damages. However, some risks such as flooding or earthquakes may require separate policies, depending on location.

Auto insurance is another essential form of property and casualty coverage. It protects against financial loss from car accidents, including vehicle repairs, medical expenses, and liability claims. Auto insurance policies often include liability coverage, collision coverage, and comprehensive coverage.

Liability coverage pays for damages if you are at fault in an accident. Collision coverage pays for repairs to your vehicle after a crash. Comprehensive coverage covers damage from non-collision events such as theft, vandalism, or weather-related incidents.

Understanding deductibles is an important part of managing property and casualty insurance. A deductible is the amount you pay out of pocket before insurance covers the rest. Higher deductibles usually lower monthly premiums, but they also increase the amount you must pay during a claim. Choosing the right deductible depends on your ability to handle unexpected costs.

Mitigating Liability Risks

Liability risks can be some of the most financially damaging because they involve legal responsibility. If you are found responsible for causing injury to another person or damaging their property, you may face lawsuits, legal fees, and settlement costs that can drain your savings or even lead to bankruptcy. Liability insurance exists to protect you from these risks.

Personal liability coverage is often included in homeowners or renters insurance policies. It can cover legal costs and damages if someone is injured on your property or if you accidentally cause harm to someone else. For example, if a visitor slips and falls in your home, liability coverage can help pay medical bills and legal expenses.

Auto insurance also includes liability coverage, which is legally required in many places. This protects you if you cause an accident that results in injury or property damage. Without liability insurance, you may be personally responsible for medical costs, vehicle repairs, and legal claims.

Umbrella insurance provides additional liability coverage beyond the limits of standard policies. It is designed for individuals with significant assets or higher risk exposure. Umbrella insurance can be especially useful for homeowners, business owners, or individuals who want added protection against major lawsuits. It offers an extra layer of financial security and is often more affordable than people expect.

Insurance as a Foundation of Financial Stability

Insurance is not just a financial product—it is a long-term strategy for protecting your future. A strong insurance plan ensures that unexpected events do not destroy your progress. It allows you to focus on building wealth, saving, and investing without constant fear of what could go wrong. While paying premiums may feel like an ongoing expense, the cost of being uninsured can be far greater.

Choosing the right insurance requires careful evaluation of your needs and your risk exposure. Too little coverage can leave you vulnerable, while too much coverage can strain your budget unnecessarily. The key is balance. Insurance should provide enough protection to prevent financial devastation while remaining affordable and aligned with your lifestyle.

When insurance is approached with understanding and strategy, it becomes a powerful tool for financial security. It protects your family, your health, your assets, and your future. By learning how insurance works and choosing coverage wisely, you strengthen your overall financial foundation and create a safety net that supports long-term stability and peace of mind.

Insurance Essentials for Financial Security in Canada

Insurance plays a major role in financial stability for Canadians, but the Canadian insurance landscape is shaped by unique systems, government programs, and provincial differences. While the core purpose of insurance remains the same—protecting against financial loss—Canadians must understand how public healthcare, provincial auto insurance laws, and federal benefit programs affect the types of coverage they truly need. In Canada, having the right insurance is not just about being responsible. It is often the difference between recovering quickly from a crisis or experiencing long-term financial damage.

Many Canadians assume they are "fully covered" because of public services like Medicare. However, Canada's public systems do not cover everything. Insurance is still essential for income protection, prescription costs, disability, home ownership risks, liability lawsuits, and long-term care needs. Building a complete Canadian financial plan means understanding which risks are covered by government programs and which risks remain your responsibility.

The Canadian Insurance System: Provincial Differences Matter

One important reality in Canada is that insurance is not uniform across the country. Many forms of insurance are regulated at the provincial level, which means the rules, required coverage, and pricing can vary depending on where you live. For example, auto insurance requirements in Ontario differ from those in Nova

Scotia, Alberta, or British Columbia. In some provinces, auto insurance is handled by a government-run provider, while in others it is private.

This means Canadians must avoid assuming that insurance advice is universal. A policy that makes sense in one province may be unnecessary—or even unavailable—in another. Your coverage should always reflect your province's laws, your local risk factors, and your personal lifestyle.

Health Insurance in Canada: What Medicare Covers and What It Doesn't

Canada's public healthcare system provides significant protection, but it does not eliminate the need for insurance. Provincial healthcare plans cover many medical services such as doctor visits and hospital stays. However, many critical health expenses are only partially covered—or not covered at all.

This is where private health insurance becomes important. Canadians often require additional coverage for prescription drugs, dental care, vision care, physiotherapy, massage therapy, mental health therapy, and medical equipment. For many people, workplace benefits provide these services, but self-employed Canadians or those without employer plans may need to purchase private coverage.

Prescription drug costs are one of the biggest gaps in Canadian healthcare. While some provinces offer drug assistance programs for seniors or low-income individuals, many working Canadians still pay significant out-of-pocket costs. A serious illness requiring expensive medication can quickly become financially overwhelming without coverage.

Extended health insurance is not only about convenience—it protects savings from being drained by medical costs that fall outside the public system.

Disability Insurance: One of the Most Important Policies for Canadians

Disability insurance is often overlooked, yet it is one of the most financially critical forms of protection.

In Canada, many people assume that government programs like Employment Insurance (EI) sickness benefits or the Canada Pension Plan Disability Benefit (CPP-D) will provide enough support. In reality, these programs are limited and may not replace enough income to maintain your lifestyle.

Disability insurance protects your earning power, which is often your most valuable financial asset. If illness or injury prevents you from working, disability coverage can replace a portion of your income and prevent you from falling into debt, missing mortgage payments, or draining retirement savings early.

For Canadians, disability insurance is especially important because many households rely on two incomes, and losing even one can create immediate financial strain. It is also essential for self-employed individuals who do not have employer-sponsored disability benefits.

A strong Canadian financial plan includes disability coverage long before retirement, because the risk of disability is statistically more likely than the risk of early death.

Life Insurance Planning in Canada

Life insurance remains a cornerstone of financial security in Canada, especially for families with dependents, mortgages, or shared debt. If a spouse or parent dies unexpectedly, the financial impact can be devastating, even if the family has savings. Life insurance provides stability by replacing lost income and preventing survivors from being forced into major lifestyle changes.

In Canada, term life insurance is often the most practical choice for young families because it provides high coverage for relatively affordable premiums. Many Canadians use term life insurance to protect the years when financial responsibilities are highest, such as raising children, paying off mortgages, or supporting a spouse.

Permanent life insurance (such as whole life) is more expensive, but it can play a role in long-term estate planning, especially for Canadians with significant assets, business ownership, or large tax liabilities upon death.

Canadians must also consider that life insurance payouts are generally tax-free to beneficiaries, making life insurance a powerful financial planning tool not only for protection, but also for legacy-building.

Critical Illness Insurance: A Common Canadian Strategy

Critical illness insurance is particularly popular in Canada because it addresses a realistic gap in financial protection. Even though hospital care may be covered through provincial healthcare, a major illness can still create significant financial burdens. People often face income loss, travel costs for treatment, specialized therapies, unpaid caregiving time, or home modifications.

Critical illness insurance provides a lump-sum payment if you are diagnosed with a covered illness such as cancer, stroke, or heart attack. This money can be used for anything—mortgage payments, income replacement, or recovery expenses. For

Canadians who want extra protection but do not qualify for strong disability coverage, critical illness insurance can be an additional layer of security.

This type of coverage is especially relevant because surviving a major illness does not automatically mean financial stability. Many Canadians recover medically but struggle financially for years afterward.

Homeowners and Renters Insurance in Canada

Home insurance is essential for Canadians because housing is often the largest asset they will ever own. A fire, major water damage, theft, or storm can cause massive financial loss without insurance. Most Canadian mortgage lenders require home insurance, but even homeowners without mortgages should view it as non-negotiable.

Canadian homeowners should also pay close attention to what their policy does *not* cover. Flooding, sewer backup, and certain types of water damage often require added endorsements. This is important in

Canada, where extreme weather events, heavy rainfall, and winter-related damage can be common depending on the region.

Renters insurance is equally important, even though many renters mistakenly believe they do not need it. In Canada, a landlord's insurance covers the building, but it does not cover your belongings or protect you from liability if you accidentally cause damage. Renters insurance is often inexpensive and can protect against theft, fire, and personal liability claims.

Auto Insurance in Canada: Provincial Rules and No-Fault Systems

Auto insurance is legally required across Canada, but the structure differs depending on your province. Some provinces operate under public insurance systems, while others rely on private insurers. In addition, many provinces have variations of no-fault insurance rules, which affect how claims are handled and how injury compensation is paid.

Canadian auto insurance policies typically include liability coverage, accident benefits, collision coverage, and comprehensive coverage. Liability coverage is essential because lawsuits from accidents can result in enormous claims, especially when injuries are involved.

Because legal minimums may not provide enough protection, many Canadians increase their liability coverage to protect their assets. This becomes more important as your net worth grows. Auto insurance is not only about repairing your vehicle—it is about preventing one accident from destroying your financial future.

Liability and Umbrella Insurance in Canada

Liability insurance is a critical part of Canadian financial security, especially as lawsuits and legal settlements become increasingly expensive. Personal liability coverage is often included in home and renters insurance, but the limits may not be high enough for serious incidents.

Umbrella insurance provides additional liability coverage beyond standard policies. In Canada, umbrella insurance is commonly used by homeowners, professionals, landlords, and business owners. It offers protection if someone sues you for serious injury, property damage, or other claims that exceed your standard policy limits.

Umbrella coverage is often overlooked because it feels unnecessary—until the moment it becomes essential. For Canadians with significant assets, it can prevent a lawsuit from wiping out savings, investments, or home equity.

Travel Insurance: A Major Canadian Necessity

Travel insurance is especially important for Canadians because healthcare coverage often does not fully extend outside the province or country. Many Canadians assume provincial healthcare will protect them while traveling, but reimbursement is often limited and may not come close to covering foreign hospital costs.

A medical emergency in the United States, for example, can result in massive bills that could destroy savings. Travel insurance protects against emergency healthcare costs, trip cancellations, and unexpected travel disruptions.

For retirees who travel frequently, travel insurance is not optional—it is one of the most practical forms of financial protection.

Long-Term Care Planning in Canada

Long-term care is one of the biggest risks for Canadian retirees. While Canada has publicly supported healthcare, long-term care services such as nursing homes, assisted living, or in-home caregiving can still create serious financial strain. Availability can also vary by province, and many families are shocked by how expensive private options can be.

Some Canadians use long-term care insurance, while others plan by building investment reserves, maintaining strong savings, or using home equity strategically. Planning ahead matters because long-term care costs can drain retirement savings quickly, especially if one spouse requires extended care for years.

Long-term care planning is not only about money—it is about protecting independence and reducing the financial and emotional burden placed on family members.

Insurance as a Foundation of Canadian Financial Security

In Canada, insurance is not just a backup plan—it is a financial survival tool. Even with government supports like Medicare, CPP, and EI, Canadians still face major financial risks related to income loss, disability, property damage, liability claims, and long-term care needs. A strong insurance plan ensures that unexpected events do not destroy your savings or derail your long-term goals.

The most effective Canadian insurance strategy is balanced coverage. Too little insurance leaves you vulnerable, while too much can strain your budget unnecessarily. The goal is to protect your income, your family, your home, and your future without overpaying for coverage you do not truly need.

When Canadians treat insurance as a key part of financial planning—not just an expense—they build a stronger foundation for stability, wealth-building, and long-term peace of mind.

CREDIT MANAGEMENT AND WEALTH BUILDING

Credit management is one of the most powerful financial skills a person can develop. It influences nearly every major financial opportunity, including purchasing a home, financing a vehicle, securing business loans, renting an apartment, and even qualifying for certain jobs. While many people associate credit with debt or financial struggle, credit itself is not inherently negative. When understood and managed properly, credit becomes a tool that can support wealth building, reduce financial barriers, and unlock opportunities that might otherwise be out of reach. Learning how to manage credit effectively is not just about avoiding financial mistakes—it is about positioning yourself for long-term financial success.

At its core, credit represents trust. It is the ability to borrow money based on the belief that you will repay it responsibly. Lenders, banks, and financial institutions rely on credit histories to evaluate risk. A strong credit profile signals reliability and stability, which often results in better borrowing options, lower interest rates, and greater financial flexibility. A weak credit profile can create obstacles, leading to higher costs and limited access to loans. Because credit affects so many areas of life, mastering credit management is a critical step toward building wealth and achieving financial independence.

Understanding Credit Scores and Reports

A credit score is a numerical representation of your creditworthiness. It is used by lenders to predict how likely you are to repay borrowed money. Credit scores are calculated using information from your credit report, which is a detailed record of your borrowing history. Credit reports are compiled by credit bureaus, which collect data from banks, credit card companies, and lenders. This data includes loan balances, payment history, credit card usage, and account status.

Credit scores are typically influenced by several major factors.

Payment history is often the most significant, because consistently paying bills on time demonstrates reliability. Credit utilization, which refers to how much of your available credit you are using, also plays a major role. A person who uses a large percentage of their credit limit may appear financially strained, even if they pay on time. Length of credit history is another factor, as longer histories provide more data and often reflect stability. Credit mix, meaning the variety of credit accounts you have (such as credit cards, loans, or mortgages), can also impact your score. New credit inquiries may lower your score temporarily, as frequent borrowing attempts can suggest financial risk.

Understanding how these factors work gives you control. A credit score is not random—it is the result of specific behaviors. When you understand what influences your score, you can take intentional steps to improve it over time. Reviewing your credit report regularly is also important because errors can occur. Incorrect information, fraudulent accounts, or reporting mistakes can harm your credit profile if left unaddressed.

The Importance of Credit in Financial Planning

Credit plays a central role in financial planning because it affects how much borrowing costs you over time. Interest rates are heavily influenced by credit scores. Someone with strong credit can often qualify for lower interest rates on mortgages, car loans, and personal loans. This can save thousands—or even tens of thousands—of dollars over the life of a loan. In contrast, someone with poor credit may face higher rates, making borrowing significantly more expensive and limiting their ability to build wealth.

Credit also affects financial access. Many major purchases, such as homes, require financing. Even renting an apartment often involves a credit check. Utility companies and cell phone providers may also use credit history to determine deposits or contract eligibility. This means credit impacts not only borrowing but also everyday financial convenience.

In wealth-building strategies, credit can be a bridge between current resources and future growth. For example, financing a home allows you to build equity over time rather than paying rent indefinitely. Business loans allow entrepreneurs to invest in expansion and generate future income. Student loans, while risky if mismanaged, can also provide access to education that increases earning potential. Credit becomes a tool that supports long-term planning when it is used with discipline and purpose.

Building and Rebuilding Credit

Building credit is essential for individuals starting their financial journey, but rebuilding credit is equally important for those recovering from past mistakes. Credit problems can happen for many reasons, including unemployment, medical emergencies, divorce, or simply lack of financial knowledge. The key is understanding that credit can be repaired with consistent effort.

For those building credit for the first time, opening a secured credit card or becoming an authorized user on a responsible family member's account can be helpful. A secured credit card requires a deposit, which acts as collateral, but it still builds credit when payments are made on time. Paying bills consistently and keeping balances low are foundational habits that support credit growth.

For those rebuilding credit, the process requires patience and structure. Paying down outstanding balances, bringing overdue accounts current, and avoiding new debt traps are essential steps. Even small improvements in payment history can have long-term positive effects. Over time, responsible credit habits begin to outweigh past negative marks.

Rebuilding credit also involves understanding that recovery is gradual. Missed payments, defaults, and collections can remain on credit reports for years. However, their impact weakens over time, especially when new positive credit behaviors are established. Consistency is more powerful than quick fixes. Credit repair services may promise instant results, but true credit rebuilding comes from stable habits and responsible borrowing.

Responsible Credit Card Management

Credit cards are among the most commonly used financial tools, but they are also one of the easiest ways to fall into debt. When used responsibly, credit cards can offer major advantages. They help build credit history, provide consumer protections against fraud, and often include rewards programs such as cash back, travel points, or discounts. Many credit cards also offer benefits like extended warranties or purchase protection.

The danger comes when credit cards are treated as extra income instead of borrowed money. Carrying a balance month to month results in interest charges, which can quickly grow into long-term debt. Credit card interest rates are often high, meaning unpaid balances can become extremely expensive.

Responsible credit card management involves paying the full balance whenever possible. If that is not possible, paying more than the minimum payment reduces interest costs and speeds up debt repayment. Another important habit is keeping credit utilization low. Using a small portion of your credit limit shows lenders that you can manage credit without relying on it heavily.

Credit cards should be used as tools for convenience and financial growth, not as solutions for overspending. When credit cards are managed with discipline, they strengthen your credit profile and support financial flexibility. When mismanaged, they become one of the fastest ways to undermine financial stability.

Leveraging Credit for Wealth Building

Credit becomes a wealth-building tool when it is used strategically rather than impulsively. Wealth building often requires investments, and credit can provide access to opportunities that generate long-term returns. For example, low-interest loans can sometimes be used to invest in real estate, business development, or education. These investments may increase income or asset value over time, making borrowing worthwhile.

Real estate is one of the most common examples of credit-based wealth building. Mortgages allow individuals to purchase property without paying the full cost upfront. Over time, mortgage payments build equity, meaning you gain ownership value in the property. If property values rise, homeowners may also benefit from appreciation, increasing their net worth.

Business financing is another example. Entrepreneurs often rely on loans, lines of credit, or business credit cards to start or expand operations. If the business grows successfully, the borrowed funds can produce income far beyond the cost of repayment.

However, leveraging credit for wealth building requires careful planning. Borrowing only works when the investment produces returns greater than the cost of interest and repayment. Using credit to invest without a clear strategy can lead to financial collapse. Wealth building through credit must be approached with caution, research, and realistic expectations.

Strategic Debt Management

Debt is often seen as negative, but not all debt is harmful. Strategic debt management involves understanding the difference between good debt and bad debt. Good debt is debt that supports long-term growth, such as mortgages, business loans, or education loans that increase earning potential. Bad debt is debt that finances short-term consumption at high interest rates, such as credit card debt or payday loans.

Managing debt strategically means minimizing high-interest debt first, as it grows quickly and drains financial resources. Paying off credit card balances, consolidating debt at lower interest rates, and avoiding unnecessary borrowing are essential strategies. It also means using low-interest debt wisely when it supports wealth-building goals.

Debt management is not only about paying off balances. It is also about protecting your cash flow. A person may have manageable debt but still struggle if monthly payments consume too much income. This is why budgeting and debt-to-income awareness are crucial. The goal is to create a balance where debt supports growth without becoming a burden that limits financial freedom.

Credit and Entrepreneurship

Credit plays a major role in entrepreneurship and business growth. A strong personal credit profile can help entrepreneurs qualify for business loans, lines of credit, and financing opportunities. Many lenders evaluate personal credit when a business is new, because the company may not yet have a financial track record. This makes personal credit a key asset for anyone interested in launching a business.

Business credit is also important because it separates personal finances from business operations. Establishing business credit can improve financing opportunities, build credibility, and reduce personal financial risk. Banks and lenders often provide business credit cards, commercial loans, and business lines of credit that help manage cash flow and support expansion.

Entrepreneurs must be especially cautious with credit because business success is not guaranteed. Borrowing too aggressively can create financial strain, especially during early stages when revenue may be unstable. Responsible credit use in entrepreneurship requires careful forecasting, realistic budgeting, and strong financial planning.

When managed wisely, credit can accelerate business growth. When mismanaged, it can lead to business failure and long-term personal financial consequences. Understanding this balance is essential for entrepreneurs who want to build sustainable wealth.

Monitoring and Protecting Your Credit

Credit management does not end once you achieve a good credit score. Maintaining strong credit requires ongoing monitoring and protection. Identity theft and fraud have become increasingly common, and unauthorized accounts can damage credit quickly. Regularly checking your credit report helps you catch errors early and address suspicious activity before it becomes a major problem.

Credit monitoring tools, whether offered through banks, credit bureaus, or financial apps, can alert you to major changes such as new accounts, credit inquiries, or missed payments. These alerts provide an added layer of protection and help you respond quickly to fraud.

Protecting credit also involves safeguarding personal information. Strong passwords, secure banking habits, and caution with emails and online links reduce the risk of phishing scams. It is also important to avoid sharing sensitive financial information unless you are certain of the legitimacy of the request.

Strong credit is an asset, and like any asset, it must be protected. Monitoring your credit ensures that your financial progress remains intact and that your credit profile continues to support your long-term goals.

Credit as a Long-Term Wealth Tool

Credit management is not simply about borrowing money—it is about building financial power. When credit is handled responsibly, it reduces borrowing costs, increases access to opportunities, and supports wealth-building strategies. It creates financial flexibility and allows individuals to pursue major life goals with greater confidence.

Mastering credit requires discipline, awareness, and long-term thinking. It involves understanding how credit works, building strong habits, using credit strategically, and protecting your financial identity. When these skills are developed, credit becomes more than a score—it becomes a foundation for stability, growth, and financial independence.

EXPLORING INVESTMENT VEHICLES

Investing is not a single action—it is a system of choices. Every investor, whether beginner or experienced, must decide where to place their money, how much risk to take, and what types of assets align best with their financial goals. This chapter explores the wide range of investment vehicles available today, from traditional options like stocks and bonds to modern alternatives that provide new pathways to diversification and wealth building. Understanding investment vehicles is essential because the strength of your portfolio depends not only on how much you invest, but also on what you invest in and why.

Investment vehicles are simply the tools used to grow wealth. Some are designed for long-term growth, others for stability, and others for income generation. Each option comes with its own risks, advantages, tax implications, and liquidity considerations. A successful investor does not rely on one type of investment alone. Instead, they build a balanced portfolio that reflects their risk tolerance, time horizon, and personal financial priorities. This chapter equips you with the knowledge to evaluate different investment options and choose strategies that support long-term financial success.

Stocks: The Foundations of Equity Ownership

Stocks are one of the most widely known and commonly used investment vehicles. When you purchase a stock, you are buying ownership in a company. This ownership gives you the potential to benefit from the company's growth and profitability. Stocks have long been viewed as one of the strongest wealth-building tools available because they offer the opportunity for significant long-term returns. However, they also come with volatility, meaning their value can rise and fall quickly depending on market conditions and company performance.

Stock prices are influenced by many factors, including earnings reports, economic conditions, industry changes, consumer demand, and investor sentiment. A company that performs well may experience rising stock prices, creating capital appreciation for investors. Some companies also pay dividends, which are payments distributed to shareholders from profits. Dividend stocks can provide steady income in addition to long-term growth potential, making them attractive for investors who want both appreciation and cash flow.

Understanding stock sectors is also essential for building a strong portfolio. Stocks are often grouped into industries such as technology, healthcare, energy, consumer goods, and finance. Different sectors respond differently to economic cycles. For example, technology stocks may grow rapidly but experience greater volatility, while consumer staple stocks may remain more stable during economic downturns. Diversifying across sectors can reduce risk and prevent your portfolio from being overly dependent on one area of the economy.

Stocks can be highly rewarding, but they require patience and discipline. Many investors make mistakes by chasing trends or panic-selling during market drops. Successful stock investing often involves a long-term mindset, careful research, and the ability to tolerate market fluctuations without reacting emotionally.

Bonds: Fixed-Income Securities

Bonds are another foundational investment vehicle, often used to provide stability and income within a portfolio. When you buy a bond, you are essentially lending money to a government, municipality, or corporation. In exchange, the issuer agrees to pay you interest over a set period and return the original amount invested when the bond reaches maturity. Bonds are typically considered lower risk than stocks, though they are not risk-free.

There are several types of bonds, each with different levels of safety and return potential. Government bonds are often viewed as some of the safest because they are backed by national governments. Corporate bonds tend to offer higher interest rates, but they carry more risk because companies can experience financial trouble or default. Municipal bonds are issued by local governments and may offer tax advantages, depending on the investor's location and tax bracket.

Bonds provide a steady income stream, making them appealing to conservative investors or individuals nearing retirement. They also help reduce volatility in a portfolio because bond prices often behave differently than stock prices. However, bonds are sensitive to interest rate changes. When interest rates rise, existing bonds often decrease in value because newer bonds offer better returns. Understanding interest rate risk is essential when investing in bonds.

Bonds are often used as a stabilizing force, balancing out riskier investments like stocks. They may not provide the same long-term growth potential as equities, but they offer reliability and predictable returns that strengthen a diversified portfolio.

Mutual Funds: Pooling Resources for Diversification

Mutual funds provide investors with access to diversified portfolios without requiring them to purchase individual stocks or bonds on their own. A mutual fund pools money from many investors and uses those funds to buy a collection of assets. Mutual funds are professionally managed, meaning a fund manager selects investments and adjusts holdings based on the fund's strategy.

One of the main advantages of mutual funds is diversification. Instead of relying on the performance of one company or one bond, mutual funds spread risk across many investments. Mutual funds can focus on stocks, bonds, or a combination of both. Some funds are designed for growth, while others focus on income or stability.

Mutual funds are convenient and accessible, especially for investors who want professional management. However, they often come with fees, such as management expense ratios (MERs), which can reduce overall returns over time. Some mutual funds also have minimum investment requirements or sales charges. Understanding fund fees is critical because even small differences in costs can significantly affect long-term growth.

Choosing the right mutual fund involves evaluating performance history, management style, risk level, and fees. Mutual funds can be excellent tools for long-term investing, but investors should ensure that the fund aligns with their goals rather than simply choosing based on popularity or short-term performance.

Exchange-Traded Funds (ETFs): Flexible and Accessible Investments

Exchange-traded funds, commonly known as ETFs, have become one of the most popular investment vehicles in modern investing. ETFs combine features of both mutual funds and stocks. Like mutual funds, they hold diversified portfolios of assets. Like stocks, they trade on stock exchanges, meaning investors can buy and sell ETF shares throughout the trading day.

ETFs are often valued for their low fees, flexibility, and accessibility. Many ETFs are designed to track market indexes, such as the S&P 500, allowing investors to gain broad market exposure without having to pick individual stocks. Because ETFs often follow passive investment strategies, their management costs are usually lower than actively managed mutual funds.

ETFs also allow investors to diversify easily across different sectors, industries, countries, and asset classes. For example, investors can purchase ETFs focused on technology, healthcare, emerging markets, bonds, or real estate. This flexibility makes ETFs powerful tools for building balanced portfolios.

However, ETFs still carry market risk. Their value can fluctuate based on market conditions. Investors must also be cautious of niche ETFs that focus on narrow sectors or risky strategies, as these can be more volatile. When used strategically, ETFs provide an efficient way to diversify, reduce costs, and build wealth over time.

Real Estate Investment Trusts (REITs): Diversifying with Real Assets

Real estate investment trusts, or REITs, allow investors to gain exposure to real estate markets without directly buying property. REITs are companies that own or manage income-generating real estate, such as apartment buildings, shopping centers, office spaces, hotels, and industrial properties. Investors buy shares in a REIT, similar to buying stock, and earn returns through dividends and property value growth.

REITs are attractive because they often generate steady income. Many REITs distribute a large portion of profits to shareholders in the form of dividends, making them appealing to income-focused investors. REITs also provide diversification because real estate markets often behave differently than stock markets.

However, REITs come with risks. They are influenced by interest rates, property market conditions, and economic demand for real estate. Rising interest rates can increase borrowing costs for REIT companies and reduce investor interest in dividend-focused assets. REIT performance can also vary widely depending on the type of real estate involved.

For many investors, REITs provide a practical way to diversify into real assets while maintaining liquidity, since REIT shares can be bought and sold more easily than physical property.

Real Estate as a Financial Tool

Real estate is one of the most powerful and widely used wealth-building tools in the world. Unlike stocks or bonds, real estate is tangible, meaning it is a physical asset with practical value. Real estate can generate wealth through appreciation, rental income, and equity growth. It also offers unique tax advantages that can make it especially attractive for long-term investors.

Real estate is often viewed as a stable investment because property values tend to rise over time, particularly in growing areas. However, real estate is not risk-free. Market downturns, property damage, high maintenance costs, and tenant issues can all affect profitability. Understanding real estate requires both financial planning and practical management skills.

Real Estate Investment Strategies

There are many ways to invest in real estate, ranging from residential properties to commercial developments. One common strategy is purchasing rental properties, where the investor earns income through monthly rent payments. Another approach is house flipping, which involves buying undervalued properties, renovating them, and selling them for profit. Some investors focus on commercial real estate, such as office buildings or retail spaces, which may offer larger income potential but also require more capital and expertise.

Real estate can provide a combination of income and appreciation, making it a valuable long-term investment. Rental income can create cash flow, while property appreciation can increase net worth over time. Real estate also provides leverage opportunities, meaning investors can use borrowed money, such as mortgages, to purchase properties and build equity gradually.

Financing Real Estate Ventures

Financing plays a major role in real estate investing. Mortgages allow buyers to purchase property without paying the full cost upfront. Mortgage terms, interest rates, down payments, and loan structures all influence long-term affordability and profitability. Choosing the right mortgage requires understanding how interest affects total repayment costs and how loan terms impact monthly cash flow.

Real estate investors often use financing as a strategic advantage, but borrowing must be handled carefully. Taking on too much debt can create financial strain, especially if rental income becomes inconsistent or market values decline. Strong real estate investing requires balancing leverage with financial stability.

Real Estate Market Dynamics

Real estate markets are shaped by supply and demand, economic conditions, employment rates, and demographic trends. Growing cities with strong job markets often experience rising housing demand, leading to higher property values. Areas with declining populations or weak economies may experience slower growth or falling prices.

Market cycles are also important. Real estate tends to move through periods of growth, stability, decline, and recovery. Understanding these cycles helps investors avoid overpaying during housing booms or panic-selling during downturns. Real estate investing requires patience and the ability to evaluate long-term trends rather than short-term fluctuations.

Tax Implications of Real Estate Ownership

Real estate offers unique tax benefits that can improve overall returns. Homeowners and investors may qualify for deductions related to mortgage interest and property taxes. Real estate investors can also benefit from depreciation, which allows them to reduce taxable income by accounting for property wear and tear over time.

Rental property owners may deduct expenses such as repairs, maintenance, insurance, and management costs. These tax advantages can significantly improve profitability, but they also require careful record-keeping and understanding of tax laws. Because tax rules vary by region, many real estate investors work with tax professionals to ensure compliance while maximizing benefits.

Real Estate for Passive Income

Real estate is often promoted as a path to passive income, particularly through rental properties. When managed effectively, rental real estate can provide steady monthly income and long-term appreciation. However, rental income is not always truly passive. Property owners must handle tenant issues, maintenance, repairs, and legal responsibilities. Many investors hire property management companies to reduce workload, but this adds costs that must be factored into profitability.

Despite the challenges, real estate remains one of the most effective long-term income-building strategies. It provides both cash flow and asset growth, making it a powerful tool for financial security and wealth creation.

Building a Well-Rounded Portfolio

Understanding investment vehicles is essential for building a portfolio that supports long-term goals. Stocks provide growth potential, bonds provide stability, mutual funds and ETFs offer diversification, REITs provide real estate exposure, and physical real estate offers both income and appreciation opportunities. Each investment vehicle plays a different role, and the strongest portfolios often combine multiple options to balance risk and reward.

A successful investor does not rely on a single strategy. Instead, they build a diversified portfolio that reflects their goals, timeline, and tolerance for risk. By understanding how each investment vehicle works, you gain the ability to make informed decisions, protect your wealth, and build a financial future rooted in strategy and long-term stability.

TAX PLANNING AND OPTIMIZATION

Tax planning is one of the most powerful yet often overlooked aspects of financial management. Many people view taxes as unavoidable and assume there is little they can do beyond filing their return each year. In reality, taxes are not just a once-a-year responsibility—they are an ongoing factor that affects income, investments, savings growth, retirement planning, and wealth transfer. A well-designed tax strategy can reduce financial strain, protect your assets, and help you keep more of what you earn. Tax planning is not about avoiding taxes illegally or exploiting loopholes—it is about understanding the system and using legitimate strategies to optimize your financial position.

Effective tax planning is a long-term process. It requires awareness of how income is taxed, how deductions and credits work, and how different investment and savings vehicles affect your taxable income. Even small tax-saving decisions, repeated over time, can result in significant financial benefits. Whether you are an employee, investor, business owner, or retiree, tax optimization plays a major role in your overall financial success.

Understanding the Tax Code

To plan effectively, you must first understand the tax system itself. The tax code is a set of laws and regulations that determine how individuals and businesses are taxed. While tax codes vary by country, most systems include similar categories such as income taxes, capital gains taxes, payroll taxes, property taxes, and estate taxes. Each type of tax affects a different area of financial life, and understanding them helps you anticipate liabilities and plan ahead.

Income tax is typically the largest tax burden for most individuals. It applies to wages, salaries, self-employment income, and in some cases additional earnings such as rental income or interest income. Most income tax systems operate on a progressive structure, meaning the tax rate increases as income rises. This structure is often divided into tax brackets, where different portions of income are taxed at different rates. Understanding how brackets work is essential because many people mistakenly believe that earning more income pushes all of their earnings into a higher tax rate. In reality, only the income above a certain threshold is taxed at the higher rate.

Capital gains tax applies when you sell an investment asset, such as stocks, bonds, or real estate, for a profit. Capital gains are often taxed differently than regular income, and in many cases, long-term capital gains are taxed at a lower rate than short-term gains. This difference makes investment holding periods an important part of tax strategy.

Property taxes apply to real estate ownership and are typically assessed annually by local governments. Estate taxes may apply when wealth is transferred after death, depending on the value of the estate and the tax laws in place. Gift taxes may also exist, limiting how much wealth can be transferred during a lifetime without triggering taxation.

Understanding these categories is important because tax planning is not limited to one area. Taxes influence nearly every financial decision, from earning income to investing, purchasing property, and passing wealth to heirs. Once you understand how the system works, you can build strategies that reduce tax burdens while supporting long-term financial growth.

Strategic Tax Planning for Individuals

Tax planning for individuals begins with recognizing that your financial choices determine your taxable income. The goal is not simply to reduce taxes in one year, but to create a sustainable plan that minimizes taxes over your lifetime. Strategic tax planning involves using legal tools such as deductions, credits, tax-advantaged accounts, and income timing strategies.

One of the most effective methods of tax optimization is contributing to tax-advantaged accounts. Retirement accounts, education savings plans, and health savings plans often provide significant tax benefits. Some accounts allow contributions to be deducted from taxable income, lowering your tax bill in the present. Others allow investments to grow tax-deferred or tax-free, reducing the long-term tax impact of investment growth. These accounts are especially valuable because they combine wealth-building with tax savings.

Deductions are another key tool. Deductions reduce taxable income, meaning you pay taxes on a smaller portion of your earnings. Common deductions may include mortgage interest, charitable donations, medical expenses, and certain work-related costs, depending on the tax system. Credits, on the other hand, reduce the actual tax you owe. Credits are often more powerful than deductions because they directly lower your tax liability.

Timing also plays an important role in tax planning. Some individuals benefit from deferring income to future years, especially if they expect to be in a lower tax bracket later. Others may benefit from accelerating deductions, such as making charitable donations before year-end. Investors may use strategies like tax-loss harvesting, where investments are sold at a loss to offset gains and reduce taxable investment income.

Tax planning also includes being aware of taxable versus non-taxable income sources. Some types of income may be taxed at lower rates, while others may be tax-exempt. Understanding these differences helps you structure your financial plan in a way that reduces unnecessary taxation.

Long-term tax planning is most effective when integrated into everyday financial habits. Keeping organized records, tracking deductible expenses, and reviewing financial decisions through a tax lens can lead to significant savings over time. Tax efficiency is not about complexity—it is about consistency and awareness.

Business Tax Strategies

For business owners and entrepreneurs, tax planning becomes

even more critical. Businesses have access to deductions and credits that are not available to individuals, but they also face more complex reporting requirements. A strong business tax strategy can improve cash flow, reduce liabilities, and support long-term growth.

One of the most important decisions for entrepreneurs is choosing the right business structure. Sole proprietorships, partnerships, corporations, and limited liability companies each have different tax implications. The structure you choose affects how income is taxed, how profits are distributed, and what deductions you can claim. Choosing the wrong structure can lead to unnecessary tax burdens and reduced profitability.

Business deductions are one of the greatest advantages of entrepreneurship. Many business expenses can be deducted, including office supplies, advertising costs, business travel, equipment purchases, professional services, and employee wages. Home office deductions may apply for individuals who work from home, though these deductions must be handled carefully to ensure compliance.

Businesses may also qualify for tax credits, which can reduce taxes owed. Credits may be available for hiring employees, investing in research and development, or adopting environmentally sustainable practices. These credits can provide major financial advantages for companies that plan strategically.

Another important aspect of business tax planning is separating personal and business finances. Mixing expenses can create accounting problems and increase the risk of audits. Maintaining clear financial records and using dedicated business accounts helps protect both financial stability and legal compliance.

Business owners must also understand the relationship between personal and business taxes. Business profits may flow through to personal income, depending on the business structure. This means that personal tax planning and business tax planning must work together. A well-managed strategy considers both sides, ensuring that overall taxation is minimized without sacrificing compliance or long-term growth.

Estate Planning and Tax Implications

Estate planning is not only about deciding who receives your assets—it is also about protecting the value of what you leave behind. Without proper planning, taxes and legal costs can reduce the wealth transferred to heirs. Estate planning ensures that your legacy is preserved and that your loved ones are not burdened with financial confusion or unnecessary expenses.

Estate taxes may apply when an estate exceeds a certain value threshold. While many individuals may not reach this threshold, those with significant assets, property holdings, or business ownership must consider estate tax planning carefully. Strategies such as gifting, creating trusts, and structuring asset transfers can reduce tax burdens and improve wealth preservation.

Trusts are commonly used tools in estate planning. A trust allows assets to be managed and distributed according to your instructions. Trusts can provide privacy, protect assets from creditors, and reduce estate tax exposure in certain situations. They also allow for more control over how wealth is passed down, such as distributing assets gradually rather than all at once.

Life insurance can also play a strategic role in estate planning. In some cases, life insurance payouts provide liquidity to cover taxes or debts, preventing heirs from needing to sell assets such as property or investments to meet financial obligations. Estate planning is not only for the wealthy. Anyone with property, dependents, or long-term financial goals can benefit from having a clear estate plan in place.

Effective estate planning ensures that wealth transfer is smooth, efficient, and aligned with your wishes. It is one of the most meaningful forms of financial planning because it protects the financial well-being of future generations.

Navigating Changes in Tax Legislation

Tax laws are not fixed. They evolve based on political decisions, economic conditions, and government priorities. Changes in tax legislation can affect income tax rates, deductions, investment taxes, retirement account rules, and business incentives. For this reason, tax planning must remain flexible. A strategy that works well today may need adjustment tomorrow.

Staying informed is a critical part of long-term tax optimization. This does not mean becoming a tax expert, but it does mean paying attention to major changes that may impact your finances. Tax law updates can create new opportunities, such as expanded deductions or credits, but they can also introduce new challenges, such as increased tax rates or reduced benefits.

Working with tax professionals can be valuable, especially for individuals with complex finances. Accountants and tax advisors can help ensure compliance, identify overlooked opportunities, and adapt strategies when laws change. Tax planning is most effective when it is proactive rather than reactive. Waiting until tax season often limits options and reduces the ability to make meaningful adjustments.

Tax Planning as a Wealth-Building Strategy

Tax planning is not simply about reducing what you owe—it is about increasing your long-term financial strength. Every dollar saved through smart tax decisions is a dollar that can be invested, saved, or used to support personal goals. Over time, tax efficiency becomes a wealth-building strategy because it improves cash flow and strengthens overall financial stability.

When combined with budgeting, investing, retirement planning, and estate planning, tax optimization becomes one of the most effective tools for long-term financial success. By understanding the tax code, using strategic planning techniques, applying business tax strategies, preparing for estate transfer, and adapting to changing laws, you create a financial plan that is not only resilient but also optimized for growth.

RETIREMENT PLANNING STRATEGIES

Retirement planning is one of the most important financial responsibilities an individual can undertake. It represents the transition from earning a steady paycheck to relying on the wealth and resources you have built over decades. A strong retirement plan is not simply about saving money—it is about creating long-term financial independence, protecting your lifestyle, and ensuring peace of mind during your later years. Without a clear strategy, retirement can become financially stressful, especially as living costs rise and healthcare expenses increase. With the right planning, however, retirement can be a period of freedom, stability, and personal fulfillment.

Retirement planning is also unique because it involves long-term decision-making. Unlike short-term goals such as saving for a vacation or paying off a credit card, retirement requires thinking decades ahead. This includes anticipating inflation, managing investment risk, preparing for unexpected expenses, and creating income systems that last throughout your lifetime. This chapter explores retirement planning strategies designed to help you build a secure financial future, maximize retirement accounts, and confidently navigate the complexities of post-career financial management.

Setting Retirement Goals

The foundation of retirement planning begins with setting clear goals. Retirement is not the same for everyone. Some individuals dream of traveling the world, while others want a quiet lifestyle close to family. Some plan to retire early, while others intend to work part-time well into their later years. Defining your vision is essential because retirement planning is not only about reaching a number—it is about building the lifestyle you want to live.

A key factor in retirement goal-setting is deciding when you want to retire. Retirement age directly impacts how much time you have to save and how long your savings must last.

Retiring earlier often requires larger savings because it reduces the number of earning years and increases the number of retirement years. Retiring later may reduce pressure on savings, but it also depends on health, job availability, and personal circumstances.

Estimating retirement expenses is another crucial step. Many individuals underestimate how much they will need. Retirement expenses often include housing costs, food, utilities, transportation, insurance, leisure activities, and unexpected emergencies. Some expenses may decrease after retirement, such as commuting costs, but others may increase, particularly healthcare and long-term care.

Healthcare is one of the largest retirement concerns. As people age, medical costs often rise, and unexpected health conditions can create financial burdens. Planning for healthcare expenses ensures that medical needs do not destroy retirement savings. Retirement goals should also include considering whether you plan to relocate, downsize, travel, or support family members financially. Every lifestyle decision impacts retirement budgeting, making goal-setting one of the most important steps in building a realistic plan.

Clear retirement goals create direction. Without goals, saving can feel vague and unmotivating. With goals, retirement planning becomes a structured process, allowing you to measure progress and adjust your strategy over time.

Retirement Accounts and Investment Vehicles

Retirement accounts are among the most powerful tools available for building long-term wealth. These accounts provide tax advantages that allow investments to grow more efficiently over time. Understanding how retirement accounts work is essential because they often form the backbone of retirement savings.

Employer-sponsored retirement plans, such as 401(k) accounts, are commonly used by working individuals. These plans allow employees to contribute a portion of their paycheck into retirement savings, often with tax benefits. Many employers also offer matching contributions, which is essentially free money added to your retirement savings. Taking full advantage of employer matching programs is one of the smartest retirement strategies because it accelerates wealth-building significantly.

Individual retirement accounts (IRAs) provide additional retirement savings opportunities. Traditional IRAs often allow contributions to be tax-deductible, reducing taxable income in the present. Roth IRAs operate differently, offering tax-free withdrawals in retirement, since contributions are made with after-tax dollars. Choosing between traditional and Roth accounts depends on your current income, expected retirement tax bracket, and long-term strategy.

Retirement accounts are not only about saving money—they are about investing. Most retirement accounts allow individuals to invest in assets such as mutual funds, ETFs, stocks, and bonds. The tax advantages of retirement accounts make them ideal for long-term growth. However, contribution limits and withdrawal rules must be understood to avoid penalties.

Strategic retirement planning often involves using multiple retirement vehicles. Some individuals contribute to employer-sponsored plans, while also maintaining IRAs or other investment accounts. The goal is to maximize tax advantages while building a diversified retirement foundation.

Creating a Diversified Retirement Portfolio

A retirement portfolio is the collection of investments you rely on to build and maintain wealth over time. One of the most important principles in retirement investing is diversification. Diversification means spreading investments across different asset types, industries, and markets to reduce risk. A well-diversified portfolio is less vulnerable to major losses because it does not rely on the performance of a single investment or market sector.

Stocks often form a major part of retirement portfolios because they provide long-term growth potential. Bonds provide stability and predictable income. Cash and cash equivalents offer liquidity and protection against short-term emergencies. Some retirement portfolios may also include real estate investments or REITs for additional diversification.

Diversification must be aligned with risk tolerance and time horizon. Younger investors often take more risk by holding more stocks because they have time to recover from market downturns. Older investors nearing retirement typically reduce risk by increasing bond holdings or stable investments, since they have less time to recover from losses.

A major part of retirement portfolio management is rebalancing. Over time, some investments may grow faster than others, shifting the balance of your portfolio. Rebalancing involves adjusting your holdings to maintain your desired asset allocation. This prevents your portfolio from becoming too risky or too conservative as markets change.

Retirement investing is not about eliminating risk. Risk is necessary for growth. The key is controlling risk in a way that supports long-term stability. A diversified portfolio helps protect retirement savings from extreme volatility while still allowing wealth to grow over time.

Income Strategies in Retirement

Retirement planning does not end when you stop working. In many ways, retirement becomes even more complex because the focus shifts from accumulation to distribution. Instead of building savings, retirees must manage withdrawals carefully to ensure their money lasts.

One common retirement income strategy is systematic withdrawals. This involves withdrawing a fixed amount of money from retirement accounts each month or year. The challenge is balancing withdrawals with investment growth. Withdrawing too much too early can deplete savings, especially if markets decline. Withdrawing too little may result in an unnecessarily restrictive lifestyle. Many retirees use withdrawal guidelines, such as the "4% rule," as a starting point, but withdrawal strategies should be adjusted based on market conditions, health, and personal expenses.

Annuities are another retirement income option. An annuity is a financial product that provides guaranteed income payments, often for life. Annuities can reduce the fear of running out of money, but they also come with fees, restrictions, and varying terms. Some retirees use annuities as part of their strategy, especially if they want stable income in addition to investment withdrawals.

Retirement income planning may also include dividend income, rental income, or part-time work. Some retirees choose to maintain part-time employment not only for income, but also for social engagement and purpose. Income sources should be diversified just like investments. Relying on one income stream creates vulnerability, while multiple streams increase stability.

Another major consideration is required minimum distributions (RMDs), which apply in certain retirement accounts. These rules require retirees to withdraw minimum amounts at specific ages. Understanding withdrawal requirements is important because failing to comply can result in penalties. Retirement income strategies must account for both lifestyle needs and legal obligations.

Long-Term Care and Healthcare Planning

Healthcare is one of the most financially significant factors in retirement planning. Many individuals assume retirement costs will decrease, but healthcare expenses often rise dramatically with age. Prescription drugs, medical treatments, hospital stays, and long-term care services can create major financial burdens if not planned for.

A strong retirement plan includes healthcare budgeting. This means estimating insurance costs, out-of-pocket expenses, and emergency medical needs. Retirees should also consider the possibility of long-term care, which includes services such as nursing homes, assisted living facilities, and in-home caregiving. Long-term care can be extremely expensive, and many people underestimate how quickly these costs can drain savings.

Long-term care insurance is one option for managing this risk. It provides financial support for care services, reducing the burden on personal savings. However, long-term care insurance policies vary widely, and premiums can be expensive. Deciding whether to purchase long-term care insurance requires evaluating personal health history, family longevity, financial resources, and risk tolerance.

Healthcare planning also includes maintaining good health habits. While no one can prevent aging, preventative care and healthy lifestyle choices can reduce long-term medical expenses and improve quality of life. Retirement planning is not only financial—it is also about protecting well-being.

Building a Retirement Plan That Lasts

Retirement planning is not a one-time task. It is an evolving process that must adapt to changing life circumstances, market conditions, and personal priorities. Income changes, job transitions, family responsibilities, economic downturns, and unexpected health events can all affect retirement strategies. This is why regular review and adjustment are essential.

Successful retirement planning combines clear goal-setting, strategic saving, diversified investing, and disciplined withdrawal strategies. It also requires planning for risks such as inflation, healthcare costs, and market volatility. Retirement is not just about reaching a certain age—it is about building financial freedom and creating the ability to live with stability and dignity.

With thoughtful planning, retirement becomes more than an ending to your career. It becomes the reward for years of preparation, discipline, and smart financial decision-making. By applying the strategies outlined in this chapter, you position yourself to achieve a retirement that is not defined by financial stress, but by independence, security, and the ability to enjoy the life you have worked so hard to build.

Retirement Planning Strategies in Canada

While the principles of retirement planning are universal, Canadians face a unique retirement landscape shaped by government programs, tax-advantaged accounts, and province-specific healthcare realities. A strong Canadian retirement plan often involves combining personal savings with federal benefits such as the Canada Pension Plan (CPP) and Old Age Security (OAS), while maximizing registered accounts like the RRSP and TFSA. Understanding how these systems work together is essential for building long-term financial stability and avoiding costly mistakes.

In Canada, retirement planning is not only about building wealth—it is also about timing withdrawals properly, minimizing taxes, and ensuring that government benefits are protected rather than reduced through poor planning. A well-structured plan allows retirees to maintain their lifestyle while managing inflation, rising housing costs, and potential long-term care needs.

Understanding Canada's Retirement Income System (CPP and OAS)

Canada's retirement system is built on a foundation of government support, but these benefits are not designed to fully replace employment income. They are meant to provide baseline stability, meaning most Canadians must still rely heavily on personal savings and investments.

The Canada Pension Plan (CPP) is funded through contributions made during your working years. The amount you receive depends on how long you contributed and how much you earned. One of the most important strategic decisions with CPP is timing. Canadians can begin receiving CPP as early as age 60, but taking it early reduces the monthly payment permanently. Delaying CPP until age 70 increases the benefit significantly. Many Canadians choose early CPP out of necessity, but those who can delay may strengthen their long-term retirement income and reduce the risk of outliving their savings.

Old Age Security (OAS) is another key income source, funded through general tax revenues rather than personal contributions. OAS is available starting at age 65, and like CPP, it can be delayed for a higher monthly payment. However, Canadians must be aware of the OAS clawback, also called the OAS recovery tax. High-income retirees may have part of their OAS reduced if their income exceeds a certain threshold. This is why tax planning becomes essential, because withdrawals from RRSPs and other taxable income sources can unintentionally trigger clawbacks.

For many Canadians, CPP and OAS provide stability, but they should be treated as only one piece of the retirement income puzzle—not the full solution.

RRSP Planning Strategies for Canadians

The Registered Retirement Savings Plan (RRSP) is one of Canada's most powerful retirement tools because it allows individuals to contribute pre-tax income, reducing taxable income in the year of contribution. Investments inside an RRSP grow tax-deferred, which means you don't pay tax until you withdraw the funds.

One of the strongest Canadian retirement strategies is maximizing RRSP contributions during high-income years. This provides larger tax refunds, allowing individuals to reinvest the refund or use it to pay down debt. RRSP contributions can be especially beneficial for Canadians in higher tax brackets, since the tax deduction is more valuable when income is higher.

However, RRSP withdrawals are taxed as income, which means the RRSP can become a tax burden if withdrawals are not planned carefully. At age 71, an RRSP must be converted into a Registered Retirement Income Fund (RRIF) or used to purchase an annuity. RRIFs come with mandatory minimum withdrawals, which can push retirees into higher tax brackets later in life.

Strategic Canadians often consider drawing down RRSPs earlier in retirement, particularly in years where their income is low, to reduce future tax pressure and minimize the risk of OAS clawbacks.

TFSA Retirement Strategies in Canada

The Tax-Free Savings Account (TFSA) is one of the most valuable retirement tools Canadians have, and its benefits are often underestimated. Unlike an RRSP, TFSA contributions are not tax-deductible, but investment growth and withdrawals are completely tax-free.

A TFSA can be a powerful retirement strategy because withdrawals do not count as taxable income. This means TFSA withdrawals do not reduce government benefits and do not contribute to OAS clawback calculations. For retirees concerned about keeping taxes low, the TFSA becomes an essential account for maintaining flexibility and protecting retirement income.

TFSAs are also ideal for emergency savings in retirement. Many retirees fear unexpected costs such as home repairs, vehicle replacement, or medical expenses. Having a TFSA allows access to funds without triggering tax consequences.

For Canadians, balancing RRSP and TFSA savings is often the best strategy, since one provides tax relief now and the other provides tax relief later.

Employer Pension Plans in Canada

Many Canadians have workplace pension plans, which can significantly strengthen retirement security. These plans typically fall into two categories: Defined Benefit (DB) and Defined Contribution (DC).

A Defined Benefit pension provides predictable retirement income based on years of service and salary history. DB pensions are highly valuable because they reduce the need for retirees to rely heavily on investments or withdrawal strategies. Canadians with DB pensions often have a more stable retirement, but they must still plan around taxation and government benefits.

A Defined Contribution pension works more like a personal investment account. Contributions are made by the employee and sometimes matched by the employer, but the final retirement income depends on investment performance. Canadians with DC pensions need strong portfolio planning and risk management, because market downturns can directly impact retirement income.

Understanding which type of pension you have is critical because it affects how much personal saving is needed and how retirement income should be structured.

Canadian Retirement Tax Planning and Withdrawal Order

One of the most overlooked retirement strategies in Canada is deciding which accounts to withdraw from first. Poor withdrawal planning can cause retirees to pay unnecessary taxes, lose government benefits, or run out of money faster than expected.

In Canada, withdrawals from RRSPs and RRIFs are fully taxable. Non-registered investments may trigger capital gains taxes. TFSA withdrawals remain tax-free. This creates opportunities for careful planning.

Many retirees benefit from a blended strategy, drawing from taxable accounts and RRSPs while preserving TFSA funds for later years. Others may choose to withdraw RRSP funds earlier to avoid large RRIF withdrawals later in life. There is no single perfect formula, but the most successful Canadian retirement plans are designed with taxation in mind.

Tax planning also matters because Canada has progressive tax brackets, meaning that higher income is taxed at higher rates. Spreading withdrawals over time can reduce the chance of jumping into higher tax brackets.

Retirement Planning for Canadians: Housing and Downsizing Considerations

Housing plays a major role in retirement planning for Canadians, especially as real estate prices continue to rise in many parts of the country. For many Canadians, their home becomes their largest asset. Retirement planning must account for mortgage costs, property taxes, insurance, and maintenance.

Downsizing is a common Canadian retirement strategy. Selling a large family home and purchasing a smaller property can free up significant funds for retirement. In Canada, the principal residence exemption often allows homeowners to sell their primary residence without paying capital gains tax, making real estate a particularly powerful wealth tool.

However, downsizing does not always guarantee savings. Some retirees underestimate moving costs, condo fees, property taxes in new areas, and the rising costs of housing even in smaller markets. A realistic retirement plan should carefully compare long-term housing expenses rather than assuming downsizing automatically solves financial pressure.

Healthcare and Long-Term Care Planning in Canada

Canada's public healthcare system reduces some retirement costs compared to other countries, but it does not eliminate them. Many services still create financial strain for retirees, including prescription drugs, dental care, vision care, mobility aids, and private home support services.

Long-term care is also a serious issue in Canadian retirement planning. Nursing homes, assisted living, and private in-home care can become expensive quickly. While some government support exists, the quality and availability of care can vary by province, and waitlists can be long.

Many Canadian retirees prepare for this risk by building a dedicated emergency fund, maintaining a TFSA for unexpected health expenses, or purchasing insurance products that support long-term care planning.

Retirement is not only about income—it is also about ensuring dignity and stability if health declines.

Retirement Planning for Canadian Couples (Income Splitting Strategies)

Canadian couples often have additional retirement planning advantages because of tax strategies such as pension income splitting. Depending on the type of pension or RRIF income received, couples may be able to shift income between spouses to reduce overall tax liability.

This is especially important when one spouse has a significantly larger RRSP or pension. If all retirement income is taxed in one person's name, that individual may face a higher tax bracket while the other spouse remains in a lower bracket. Income splitting can reduce the household tax burden and help preserve government benefits like OAS.

Canadian retirement planning is strongest when couples coordinate savings, withdrawals, and long-term care planning together instead of treating retirement as an individual financial issue.

Building a Canadian Retirement Plan That Lasts

Retirement planning in Canada requires more than saving money—it requires understanding how personal savings interact with government programs, taxation rules, and long-term healthcare realities. CPP and OAS provide important support, but they are rarely enough to fully fund retirement. This is why RRSPs, TFSAs, pensions, and personal investments must be built into a complete strategy.

A strong Canadian retirement plan is built through clear goal-setting, disciplined saving, smart investing, and careful withdrawal planning. It also includes tax awareness, housing decisions, and preparation for long-term care costs. Canadians who regularly review their plan and adjust for life changes are far more likely to retire with confidence and stability.

With the right strategy, retirement in Canada can become not only financially secure, but personally fulfilling—allowing individuals to enjoy the freedom, comfort, and peace of mind they have worked decades to achieve.

ENTREPRENEURSHIP IN THE FINANCIAL SECTOR

Entrepreneurship provides individuals with a powerful opportunity to take control of their financial future, build wealth, and create meaningful impact. Within the financial sector, entrepreneurship becomes especially significant because the financial services industry influence nearly every aspect of modern life. From banking and investing to insurance, lending, and digital payments, financial systems shape how people build stability, manage risk, and pursue long-term goals. Entrepreneurs who enter the financial sector have the potential to create innovative solutions that improve access, efficiency, and financial empowerment for individuals and businesses.

The financial industry is also one of the most dynamic and rapidly evolving markets in the world. Technology, globalization, and shifting consumer expectations have transformed how the financial services industry is delivered. Traditional banking models are being challenged by FinTech startups, digital payment systems, and decentralized financial platforms. At the same time, financial consumers are demanding faster services, better transparency, and more personalized experiences. These changes have created a strong environment for innovation and new business opportunities.

However, entrepreneurship in the financial sector also carries unique challenges. Financial businesses must operate in heavily regulated environments, handle sensitive customer information, and maintain strong ethical practices. Trust is essential in finance. Unlike many other industries, financial entrepreneurs are often responsible for managing other people's money, data, or security. This creates high expectations and high consequences for mistakes. Successful financial entrepreneurship requires creativity, strong business planning, regulatory awareness, and disciplined risk management. This chapter explores the major components of building a financial venture and provides insight into how entrepreneurs can thrive in this competitive and high-stakes field.

Identifying Entrepreneurial Opportunities

The first step in financial entrepreneurship is identifying an opportunity that solves a real problem. The financial services industry is deeply connected to human needs, which means opportunities often arise where people feel frustrated, underserved, or excluded. Many financial products are complex, expensive, or difficult to access. Entrepreneurs who can simplify processes, reduce barriers, or improve user experiences often find strong demand.

FinTech is one of the fastest-growing areas for financial entrepreneurship. FinTech businesses create digital tools that improve banking, lending, investing, budgeting, and payments. Mobile banking apps, automated investing platforms, peer-to-peer payment systems, and digital lending services are examples of

FinTech innovation that have already reshaped consumer finance. Despite rapid growth, FinTech continues to offer new opportunities, especially in areas such as financial inclusion, fraud prevention, and personalized wealth management.

Niche The financial services industry also provide strong entrepreneurial potential. Many communities and industries have specific financial needs that are not fully addressed by traditional institutions. Entrepreneurs may create specialized services such as financial coaching for young professionals, debt reduction consulting, tax advisory firms for small businesses, or insurance solutions for emerging industries. These niche services can thrive because they offer expertise and tailored solutions rather than generic financial products.

Another major opportunity exists in education and financial literacy. Millions of people struggle with budgeting, credit management, investing, and retirement planning because they were never taught these skills. Entrepreneurs who build financial education platforms, coaching programs, or digital learning tools can create both profit and social impact. Financial literacy businesses often succeed because they meet a widespread demand while building trust and long-term customer relationships.

The most successful entrepreneurial opportunities often come from personal experience. Many entrepreneurs build businesses based on challenges they have faced themselves, such as struggling with debt, managing complex taxes, or navigating investment confusion. When entrepreneurs understand the problem deeply, they are better positioned to create solutions that truly meet customer needs.

Building a Business Plan for Financial Ventures

A strong business plan is essential for launching any financial venture, but it is especially important in the financial sector due to the complexity and trust-based nature of the industry. A business plan serves as a blueprint that outlines what your business will do, how it will operate, and how it will generate profit. It also helps you evaluate whether your idea is realistic, scalable, and sustainable.

The first key component of a business plan is market analysis. This involves researching the target audience, understanding customer needs, and evaluating competitors. In the financial sector, competition can come from traditional banks, large financial firms, and emerging startups. Entrepreneurs must identify what differentiates their service and why customers would choose their solution over existing options. Market research helps clarify demand and ensures the business idea is grounded in real consumer needs rather than assumptions.

A strong financial business plan also includes a clear revenue model. Financial businesses can generate revenue through service fees, subscription models, commissions, transaction fees, interest-based lending, or premium product offerings. Choosing the right revenue model depends on the type of business being built. For example, a FinTech budgeting app may rely on subscription fees, while a lending business may earn profits through interest. Entrepreneurs must carefully evaluate revenue streams because profitability is often tied directly to regulatory compliance, customer trust, and long-term retention.

Scalability is another crucial element. Some financial businesses are designed to grow rapidly, such as digital platforms that can expand to thousands of users. Others may grow slowly but steadily, such as boutique advisory firms. Entrepreneurs must decide whether their venture is intended to remain local and specialized or expand nationally and globally. Scalability influences staffing, technology investments, marketing strategies, and funding needs.

Finally, a business plan should outline operational strategies. This includes staffing requirements, technology needs, marketing approaches, customer acquisition strategies, and projected expenses. Financial businesses often require strong customer support systems because clients need guidance and reassurance when dealing with money. Entrepreneurs who plan for customer experience from the beginning often build stronger reputations and long-term trust.

Navigating Regulatory Compliance

Regulatory compliance is one of the defining challenges of entrepreneurship in the financial sector. The financial services industry is heavily regulated because they directly impact consumer protection, economic stability, and fraud prevention. Entrepreneurs must understand that operating without proper licensing or compliance can result in severe penalties, lawsuits, or business closure.

Regulations vary depending on the type of financial service offered. Businesses involved in lending, investment advising, insurance, and banking often require specific licenses and must follow strict legal guidelines. Compliance requirements may include reporting standards, transparency obligations, anti-money laundering measures, consumer privacy protections, and ethical marketing rules. Entrepreneurs must understand these requirements before launching their business.

One of the most critical aspects of compliance is protecting customer information. Financial businesses often handle sensitive data such as social insurance numbers, bank account details, credit history, and transaction records. Regulations related to privacy and cybersecurity are strict because data breaches can destroy consumer trust and cause devastating financial harm.

Entrepreneurs must also remain adaptable because financial regulations change frequently. Governments introduce new rules in response to economic shifts, emerging technologies, and financial crises. Staying informed about regulatory updates is essential for long-term success. Many financial entrepreneurs work with legal professionals, compliance officers, or regulatory consultants to ensure their business remains compliant as it grows.

Compliance should not be viewed as an obstacle—it should be viewed as part of building credibility. Customers trust financial businesses that demonstrate transparency, professionalism, and legal integrity. Strong compliance practices build a foundation for long-term stability and brand trust.

Leveraging Technology for Financial Innovation

Technology has become one of the most powerful forces shaping modern finance. Entrepreneurs who understand technology have a major advantage because digital innovation can reduce costs, increase efficiency, and improve customer experiences. FinTech tools have already transformed banking and investing, and the next wave of innovation is expected to reshape the financial services industry even further.

Artificial intelligence is increasingly used in fraud detection, customer service automation, credit scoring, and investment management. AI-driven systems can analyze customer behavior, identify suspicious transactions, and provide personalized recommendations. This allows financial businesses to improve efficiency while also offering more customized services.

Blockchain technology has introduced new possibilities for secure and transparent transactions. It has been used in Cryptocurrency markets, decentralized finance platforms, and digital asset tracking. While blockchain is still evolving, it has the potential to reduce transaction costs, improve security, and create new financial ecosystems.

Automation is another major advantage. Many financial entrepreneurs build systems that automate budgeting, bill payments, investing, or financial reporting. Automation improves convenience for customers while reducing workload for businesses. Digital tools can also improve accessibility, allowing individuals in remote areas or underserved communities to access the financial services industry without relying on traditional institutions.

However, technology also introduces risks. Digital financial platforms must prioritize cybersecurity, system reliability, and user trust. A single system failure or security breach can permanently damage a business. Financial entrepreneurs must balance innovation with responsibility, ensuring that technology strengthens customer protection rather than creating vulnerabilities.

Managing Risks in Financial Entrepreneurship

Risk management is essential in any business, but it is especially critical in financial entrepreneurship. Financial businesses are exposed to risks that can threaten both profitability and reputation. These risks include cybersecurity threats, regulatory violations, economic downturns, market volatility, and consumer trust issues.

Cybersecurity risk is one of the largest threats facing financial entrepreneurs. Digital platforms are frequent targets for hackers, and financial data is among the most valuable information criminals can steal. Entrepreneurs must invest in strong security systems, encryption, fraud monitoring, and employee training to reduce vulnerabilities. Cybersecurity is not optional in finance—it is a core requirement for survival.

Economic and market risks also impact financial ventures. Lending businesses may face higher default rates during recessions. Investment platforms may struggle during market downturns when clients become fearful. Even financial advisory services may face reduced demand when consumers cut back on spending. Entrepreneurs must plan for economic uncertainty and build financial resilience into their business model.

Reputational risk is another major concern. Financial businesses depend on trust. Customers must believe that the business is secure, honest, and competent. Even small mistakes, such as unclear pricing or poor customer service, can damage reputation. Transparency and ethical practices are essential for building credibility.

Entrepreneurs must also manage operational risk, including staffing challenges, system failures, and poor financial planning. Many startups fail not because the idea is bad, but because operations are disorganized or cash flow is mismanaged. Strong internal systems, careful budgeting, and strategic growth planning reduce these risks.

Entrepreneurship as a Pathway to Financial Impact

Entrepreneurship in the financial sector is both challenging and rewarding. It requires a strong balance of creativity, business strategy, compliance awareness, and risk management. Financial entrepreneurs have the opportunity to build profitable businesses while also contributing to broader financial empowerment. They can help individuals gain access to banking services, improve financial literacy, build credit, invest wisely, and protect their futures.

The financial sector will continue evolving, creating new opportunities for those willing to innovate. Entrepreneurs who remain adaptable, ethical, and customer-focused can build ventures that not only generate wealth but also create meaningful change. Financial entrepreneurship is not simply about building a business—it is about shaping how people interact with money, security, and opportunity in a world where The financial services industry play an increasingly central role.

Financial Entrepreneurship in Canada: A Unique Opportunity

Entrepreneurship in Canada's financial sector offers a powerful pathway to wealth-building because the demand for financial guidance is growing rapidly. Canadians are facing higher housing costs, rising consumer debt, inflation pressure, and increasing retirement uncertainty. At the same time, many Canadians still lack strong financial literacy and do not have access to personalized financial advice.

This creates a major opportunity for entrepreneurs to build businesses around financial education, insurance planning, investment services, and debt management. In Canada, financial entrepreneurship is especially valuable because it can be structured as a flexible career path, allowing individuals to build income part-time or full-time while developing long-term clients and referral networks.

Unlike traditional businesses that require inventory, storefronts, or large startup capital, many financial service ventures can be launched with relatively low overhead—provided the entrepreneur is willing to commit to licensing, training, compliance, and ethical responsibility.

Common Canadian Entry Paths into Financial Entrepreneurship

In Canada, entrepreneurship in the financial services industry often begins through one of three pathways:

Some individuals build independent advisory practices, usually requiring licensing and often working through a brokerage or insurance MGA (Managing General Agency). This path offers flexibility but requires strong compliance awareness, marketing skill, and professional credibility.

Others choose FinTech entrepreneurship, building apps or platforms for budgeting, lending, investing, and digital payments. This path is scalable but often requires significant technical expertise and regulatory planning.

A third pathway involves partnering with established financial organizations that provide training, licensing support, and product access. This is where companies like Primerica[i] become relevant as a structured option for entry-level entrepreneurs.

Primerica as a Business Model in Financial Entrepreneurship

Primerica is widely known in Canada and the United States as a company that provides individuals with a business opportunity in financial services, primarily focused on term life insurance and financial education. For many people, Primerica represents a low-barrier entry point into the industry because it provides structured training, a system for prospecting, and a recognizable brand.

For aspiring entrepreneurs who do not have prior finance experience, this type of organization can be appealing because it offers a framework and community support that reduces the intimidation factor of entering a complex industry.

Primerica is often described as a business opportunity that blends the financial services industry with a recruiting-driven model, meaning that individuals may earn income through personal sales and also through building a team. This approach is not for everyone, but it can be effective for those who are comfortable with networking, sales communication, and leadership development.

However, success in this model depends heavily on personal effort, ethical selling, transparency, and long-term client trust.

Benefits of a Structured Organization Like Primerica

One of the strongest advantages of joining an organization like Primerica is that it provides a clear starting point. Many people want to enter The financial services industry but do not know where to begin. A structured company can provide step-by-step guidance, mentorship, and licensing direction.

Another benefit is that entrepreneurs can often begin with limited startup costs compared to launching an independent financial firm. Rather than building a business completely from scratch, the entrepreneur gains access to training systems, product infrastructure, and a network-driven approach to client acquisition.

For individuals who are motivated, disciplined, and people-oriented, this can create a realistic path toward building income, developing leadership experience, and eventually transitioning into a long-term career in financial services.

Important Ethical Considerations for Primerica and Similar Models

While structured organizations offer opportunities, financial entrepreneurship must always be approached ethically—especially when income depends on commissions and recruiting.

In Canada, consumers are increasingly cautious about financial sales models, and many people distrust companies that appear overly recruitment-focused. Because of this, any entrepreneur working through Primerica (or any similar organization) must prioritize professional conduct and avoid aggressive sales tactics.

The biggest long-term risk in a recruiting-driven model is reputational damage. If clients feel pressured, misled, or treated like a transaction, the business will struggle to survive. Trust is the currency of financial entrepreneurship. The entrepreneur must always present products clearly, explain costs and limitations honestly, and focus on client outcomes rather than short-term commission.

In the financial sector, ethical failure is not a minor mistake—it can destroy credibility permanently.

Licensing and Compliance in Canada (Critical for All Financial Entrepreneurs)

In Canada, selling insurance or providing investment guidance is regulated provincially and federally depending on the product. Financial entrepreneurs must meet licensing requirements, follow compliance rules, and understand consumer protection obligations.

This is especially important for new entrants who may not realize how serious compliance is. Entrepreneurs must ensure that they are properly licensed before offering advice, selling products, or representing themselves as financial professionals.

Companies like Primerica often support licensing preparation and training, but the responsibility still falls on the individual. In Canada, regulatory bodies and provincial insurance councils enforce rules strictly, and violations can lead to penalties, license suspension, or legal consequences.

A true financial entrepreneur treats compliance as part of their professional identity, not as a checklist.

Financial Entrepreneurship in Canada: Best Practices for Long-Term Success

Whether an entrepreneur builds an independent practice, launches a FinTech product, or joins a structured company like Primerica, the foundation of success is the same: trust, education, and client value.

The most sustainable financial entrepreneurs build their businesses by focusing on long-term relationships instead of short-term transactions. They prioritize financial literacy, helping clients understand budgeting, debt reduction, protection planning, and retirement strategies.

In Canada, this approach is especially valuable because many families feel overwhelmed by rising costs and uncertainty. Entrepreneurs who can simplify financial planning and provide clear guidance can create massive impact—and build profitable businesses at the same time.

Entrepreneurship in the Financial Sector as a Wealth-Building Career

Entrepreneurship in finance is not simply about selling products. It is about creating a business that solves real financial problems, protects families, and improves long-term stability.

Organizations like Primerica represent one possible entry point into this world, particularly for individuals who want a guided structure, training support, and a relationship-based model. For some entrepreneurs, it can be a strong stepping stone into the financial industry. For others, an independent or FinTech-driven path may be a better fit.

Ultimately, the best option depends on the individual's personality, ethics, long-term goals, and willingness to build credibility through education and professionalism.

In Canada's evolving economy, financial entrepreneurship remains one of the most powerful opportunities available—because money management, protection planning, and financial literacy will always be in demand.

RISK MANAGEMENT IN FINANCIAL SERVICES

Risk is an unavoidable reality in the financial world. Every financial decision—whether made by an individual investor, a business owner, or a major financial institution—carries some degree of uncertainty. Markets fluctuate, borrowers default, economic conditions shift, and unexpected crises can disrupt even the most carefully designed plans. For this reason, risk management is not simply a specialized topic reserved for banks and professional investors. It is a core financial skill that influences stability, long-term success, and wealth preservation.

In financial services, risk management refers to the systems, strategies, and decision-making processes used to identify potential threats, measure their impact, and reduce the likelihood of severe financial loss. Risk cannot be eliminated completely, but it can be managed intelligently. Strong risk management allows individuals and institutions to protect assets, maintain stability during uncertainty, and make decisions that balance growth with security. Without risk management, even high-income earners and successful businesses can experience sudden financial collapse.

This chapter explores the key types of financial risks, the methods used to measure and assess them, the tools used to mitigate risk, the role of regulation, and the importance of crisis preparedness. Understanding these concepts strengthens your ability to navigate financial uncertainty with discipline and confidence.

Types of Financial Risks

Financial risks come in many forms, and understanding their differences is essential for developing effective strategies. Each type of risk affects financial stability in a unique way, and many risks overlap, meaning one event can trigger multiple problems at once.

Market risk is one of the most widely recognized financial risks. It refers to the possibility of financial loss due to changes in market conditions, such as stock price declines, interest rate changes, or shifts in currency exchange rates. Investors face market risk when holding stocks, bonds, mutual funds, or other traded assets. Market risk is influenced by economic cycles, political instability, inflation, global crises, and investor sentiment. Even strong investments can lose value temporarily during market downturns, making market risk an unavoidable part of investing.

Credit risk refers to the risk that a borrower will fail to repay a loan. Banks face credit risk when issuing mortgages, business loans, and credit card debt. Individuals also face credit risk when lending money privately or investing in bonds. Credit risk increases during economic recessions, when unemployment rises and businesses struggle to generate revenue. A rise in loan defaults can weaken banks, reduce lending availability, and create widespread economic stress.

Liquidity risk is the risk of being unable to access cash quickly without suffering significant loss. Some assets, such as real estate or private business investments, may have high value but cannot be sold easily. Liquidity risk becomes a serious issue during emergencies when immediate funds are needed. Even financial institutions face liquidity risk if too many customers withdraw deposits at the same time.

Operational risk involves failures within internal systems, processes, or human decision-making. This includes errors in accounting, fraud committed by employees, technology breakdowns, or poor management decisions. Operational risk is often underestimated, yet it can be highly damaging. A single security breach or internal failure can cause massive financial loss and reputational damage.

Regulatory risk refers to the potential impact of changes in laws or regulations. Financial institutions must comply with strict legal standards. When regulations shift, businesses may face new reporting requirements, higher costs, or restrictions on certain activities. Regulatory risk can also affect individuals, particularly when tax laws, investment rules, or retirement regulations change.

Reputational risk is another major factor, particularly in the financial sector where trust is everything. Financial institutions rely on customer confidence. A scandal, fraud case, or major customer service failure can destroy credibility, leading to lost clients and long-term financial harm. Even individuals face reputational risk in business settings if financial decisions damage professional standing.

Geopolitical risk includes risks tied to political instability, war, trade conflicts, and global economic disruptions. These events can cause rapid market declines, currency instability, and sudden shifts in commodity prices. Geopolitical risk is difficult to predict, which makes it especially important to prepare for through diversification and long-term planning.

Understanding these risk categories allows individuals and institutions to recognize threats before they become crises. Risk management begins with awareness. If you do not understand what risks exist, you cannot plan for them effectively.

Risk Assessment and Measurement

Managing risk effectively requires accurate assessment. Risk assessment involves identifying potential threats, estimating how likely they are to occur, and evaluating the financial damage they could cause. Without measurement, risk management becomes guesswork, and guesswork is dangerous in finance.

Financial institutions often use quantitative models to measure risk exposure. These models may analyze market volatility, historical performance trends, and economic indicators. One common approach is value-at-risk (VaR), which estimates how much money could be lost in a portfolio under normal market conditions within a specific time period. While VaR is widely used, it is not perfect, because it may underestimate rare but severe market crashes.

Stress testing is another important method. Stress testing evaluates how financial portfolios or institutions would perform under extreme conditions, such as a recession, sudden interest rate spikes, or major market crashes. Stress testing helps identify vulnerabilities that may not be visible during stable economic periods.

Risk assessment is not only for institutions. Individuals can also apply risk measurement concepts. For example, an investor can evaluate how much of their wealth is exposed to stocks versus safer assets. A homeowner can assess whether their emergency fund is sufficient to handle unexpected job loss. A business owner can calculate whether they have enough cash reserves to survive a slow sales season.

Risk measurement also includes evaluating probability versus consequence. Some risks are unlikely but devastating, such as a major medical emergency or economic crash. Others are more likely but less severe, such as short-term market dips. Effective risk management balances these possibilities and prepares for both frequent disruptions and rare disasters.

Hedging and Risk Mitigation Strategies

Once risks are identified and measured, the next step is mitigation. Risk mitigation refers to actions taken to reduce the likelihood or impact of financial loss. One of the most common strategies is diversification, which spreads investments across multiple assets to reduce reliance on one market or sector. Diversification does not prevent losses, but it reduces the chance that one event will destroy an entire portfolio.

Hedging is another important strategy. Hedging involves using financial instruments to offset potential losses. Derivatives such as options and futures are commonly used for hedging. For example, an investor may purchase an option contract that increases in value if a stock declines, helping protect against market downturns. Businesses also hedge against currency risk when operating internationally, using financial contracts to stabilize exchange rate exposure.

While hedging can be powerful, it requires expertise. Derivatives can be complex and may increase risk if used incorrectly. For individuals, hedging may not always be necessary, but understanding the concept is valuable because it demonstrates how professional investors protect wealth during uncertainty.

Insurance is another major risk mitigation tool. Insurance protects against losses related to health emergencies, property damage, lawsuits, disability, and death. Insurance does not remove risk, but it transfers risk to the insurer, preventing catastrophic financial loss.

Emergency savings are also essential. Liquidity is a major form of risk protection. Having an emergency fund allows individuals to handle unexpected expenses without relying on credit cards or selling investments at a loss. For businesses, cash reserves serve the same purpose, providing stability during downturns.

Risk mitigation also involves limiting exposure to high-risk behavior. This includes avoiding excessive debt, reducing speculative investments, and ensuring financial obligations remain manageable. Many financial crises occur when people or institutions take on too much leverage, meaning they borrow heavily to increase potential returns. Leverage can magnify gains, but it also magnifies losses, making it one of the most dangerous forms of financial risk.

Regulatory Compliance and Risk

Regulation plays a major role in risk management within financial services. Governments regulate banks and financial institutions to protect consumers, reduce fraud, and prevent systemic collapse. Compliance is not simply a legal requirement—it is a form of risk protection.

Financial regulations often require banks to maintain reserve levels, disclose risks to customers, and follow strict lending standards. These regulations reduce the likelihood of reckless behavior that could destabilize the economy. Anti-money laundering laws, fraud prevention requirements, and consumer protection regulations all help reduce financial crime and unethical practices.

For financial businesses, compliance reduces legal risk, reputational risk, and operational risk. A company that violates regulations may face fines, lawsuits, and loss of credibility. Compliance also builds trust, which is essential for long-term success in finance.

For individuals, regulatory awareness is equally important. Understanding consumer rights, banking protections, and investment regulations helps individuals avoid scams and make informed financial decisions. Regulations shape the safety of deposits, the fairness of lending practices, and the transparency of investment products. Financial literacy includes knowing how these protections work and how to use them when needed.

Crisis Management and Resilience

Even with strong risk management systems, crises can still occur. Economic downturns, global pandemics, market crashes, and unexpected geopolitical events can create financial turbulence that tests the strength of institutions and individuals. Crisis management is the ability to respond effectively when disruption happens.

Financial institutions prepare for crises through contingency planning, stress testing, liquidity reserves, and emergency response protocols. During financial crises, institutions may face mass withdrawals, loan defaults, or market collapses. Those with strong crisis preparation are more likely to survive, while those with weak planning may collapse quickly.

Individuals also need crisis strategies. A personal crisis plan may include emergency savings, diversified investments, insurance coverage, and backup income sources. It may also include planning for job loss, unexpected medical expenses, or family emergencies. Crisis resilience is built through preparation, not reaction.

One of the most important lessons from past financial crises is the value of discipline. Panic-driven decision-making often worsens financial damage. Investors who sell during market crashes often lock in losses, while those who remain patient may recover as markets rebound. Businesses that cut costs strategically and maintain liquidity are more likely to survive downturns than those that rely heavily on debt.

Resilience also requires adaptability. Economic conditions change, and financial strategies must evolve. Risk management is not a one-time task—it is an ongoing process of evaluating exposure, updating strategies, and preparing for uncertainty.

Risk Management as a Financial Survival Skill

Risk management is not about eliminating uncertainty. It is about building the ability to survive and succeed in an unpredictable world. By understanding different types of financial risks, learning how to measure and assess exposure, applying mitigation strategies such as diversification and hedging, and preparing for crises, individuals and institutions can strengthen their financial stability.

In the financial services industry, risk management is a foundation for trust and long-term success. For individuals, it is a survival skill that protects wealth, prevents financial collapse, and creates confidence in decision-making. A strong financial future depends not only on growth strategies, but also on the ability to withstand challenges. Risk management provides that strength, ensuring that setbacks do not become permanent failures, and that financial stability can endure even in the most uncertain environments.

THE ROLE OF TECHNOLOGY IN FINANCE

Technology has become one of the most influential forces shaping modern finance. In past generations, The financial services industry were built around physical banks, paper records, in-person transactions, and slow processing systems. Today, the financial world moves at digital speed. Payments can be made instantly, investments can be managed through mobile apps, and loans can be approved in minutes rather than weeks. Technology has not only increased convenience—it has fundamentally changed how The financial services industry is delivered, how consumers interact with money, and how financial institutions operate in an increasingly competitive global environment.

The role of technology in finance extends far beyond online banking. Innovations such as FinTech platforms, blockchain systems, artificial intelligence, automation, and advanced cybersecurity tools are redefining the financial sector. Technology has expanded access to financial services, especially for individuals and communities previously underserved by traditional banks. It has also introduced new risks, including cybercrime, fraud, misinformation, and regulatory uncertainty. Understanding the relationship between technology and finance is essential for anyone who wants to navigate modern financial systems with confidence. This chapter explores the major technological developments transforming finance and the opportunities and challenges they create.

FinTech Revolution

The rise of financial technology, commonly known as FinTech, has disrupted traditional The financial services industry and created a new era of financial accessibility. FinTech refers to technology-driven innovations that improve or replace traditional financial systems. Over the past decade, FinTech startups have introduced services that allow consumers to send money instantly, apply for loans online, invest through automated platforms, and manage budgets with real-time tracking tools.

One of the most visible impacts of FinTech is in digital payments. Mobile payment platforms and digital wallets have made it easier than ever to transfer money without cash or checks. Peer-to-peer payment services allow individuals to send money to friends, family, and businesses instantly, reducing reliance on traditional banking transfers. These platforms have reshaped consumer expectations, making speed and convenience the new standard.

FinTech has also transformed lending. Traditional lending often requires lengthy paperwork, credit checks, and slow approval processes. FinTech lenders use digital applications and automated underwriting systems to speed up approvals and offer alternative lending options. Peer-to-peer lending platforms allow individuals to lend directly to borrowers, bypassing traditional banks. These innovations have expanded credit access, especially for those who may not qualify through conventional methods.

Another major FinTech development is robo-advising. Robo-advisors use algorithms to manage investment portfolios automatically based on an investor's goals and risk tolerance. This has made investing more affordable and accessible, especially for individuals who cannot afford traditional wealth management services. FinTech has reduced barriers to entry, allowing more people to participate in investing and financial planning.

However, FinTech disruption also creates challenges. Many FinTech companies operate with different regulations than traditional banks, raising concerns about consumer protection and data security. While FinTech increases access and convenience, it also requires consumers to be cautious, informed, and aware of potential risks. The FinTech revolution is powerful because it reshapes financial systems, but it also demands higher levels of digital literacy and personal responsibility.

Blockchain and Cryptocurrencies

Blockchain technology has introduced a new approach to financial transactions and record-keeping. Blockchain is a decentralized digital ledger that records transactions across a network of computers. Instead of relying on a central authority, such as a bank, blockchain systems rely on shared verification, transparency, and cryptographic security. This structure makes blockchain unique because it reduces the need for intermediaries and creates a system where trust is built through technology rather than centralized institutions.

Cryptocurrencies such as Bitcoin and Ethereum are among the most well-known applications of blockchain. These digital currencies allow users to send and receive money without traditional banks. Transactions are recorded on the blockchain, and ownership is verified through cryptographic keys. Cryptocurrency has gained attention as both a payment system and an investment asset, attracting individuals interested in financial independence, decentralization, and high-growth opportunities.

Blockchain technology has the potential to improve efficiency and security in finance. It can reduce transaction costs, speed up cross-border payments, and create more transparent record systems. In traditional finance, international transfers can take days and involve multiple intermediaries. Blockchain-based transfers can occur more quickly, often at lower cost. This has major implications for global trade and remittances.

However, blockchain and Cryptocurrency also come with serious challenges. Cryptocurrency markets are highly volatile, and prices can fluctuate dramatically within short periods. Security risks exist as well, including hacking, fraud, and loss of digital keys. Unlike traditional banking systems, Cryptocurrency transactions are often irreversible, meaning mistakes can lead to permanent loss of funds.

Regulatory uncertainty is another major issue. Governments worldwide are still developing rules for Cryptocurrency taxation, trading, and consumer protection. While blockchain offers innovation, it also raises questions about financial stability, illegal transactions, and investor protection. Understanding both the promise and the risks of blockchain is essential for anyone exploring its role in modern finance.

Artificial Intelligence in Finance

Artificial intelligence has become one of the most transformative technologies in financial services. AI refers to systems that can analyze data, recognize patterns, and make decisions or predictions with minimal human involvement. In finance, AI is used to automate tasks, improve efficiency, and enhance decision-making across many sectors.

One of the most common uses of AI is in fraud detection. Financial institutions process millions of transactions daily, and identifying suspicious activity manually would be impossible. AI systems analyze transaction patterns and flag unusual behavior, such as large withdrawals, international purchases, or unexpected spending habits. This allows banks to detect fraud faster and protect customer accounts more effectively.

AI is also widely used in algorithmic trading. In investment markets, AI systems analyze market trends, news events, and price movements to make trading decisions in fractions of a second. These systems can respond faster than human traders, giving financial institutions an advantage in high-speed trading environments. While algorithmic trading increases efficiency, it can also contribute to market volatility if large automated systems react to the same signals at the same time.

Risk management is another area where AI is reshaping finance. AI models help financial institutions assess credit risk by analyzing borrower data, income patterns, and financial behavior. Some systems can even incorporate alternative data sources, such as spending habits or utility payment history, to evaluate creditworthiness. This can expand access to loans for individuals who may not have traditional credit histories.

Customer service has also been transformed by AI through chatbots and automated support systems. AI-driven customer service tools provide 24/7 assistance, handle common banking questions, and reduce wait times. While this improves convenience, it can also reduce human interaction, which some customers still prefer for complex financial issues.

AI also raises ethical concerns. Automated decision-making can lead to bias if algorithms are trained on flawed or discriminatory data. Privacy is another concern, as AI systems require large amounts of personal information to function effectively. The widespread use of AI in finance creates opportunities for efficiency, but it also demands careful oversight to ensure fairness, transparency, and accountability.

Digital Transformation of Banking

Banking has experienced a major digital transformation, changing how customers interact with financial institutions. Traditional banking once relied heavily on physical branches, paper checks, and in-person customer service. Today, many banking services are delivered digitally through online platforms and mobile apps. Customers can transfer funds, pay bills, apply for loans, and deposit checks without ever entering a bank branch.

Mobile banking has increased accessibility and convenience, allowing individuals to manage their finances in real time. This has been especially beneficial for people who live far from physical branches or who have busy schedules. Digital banking also allows customers to track spending, receive transaction alerts, and automate transfers, which can improve financial awareness and budgeting.

Virtual banking services have also expanded, with many banks offering fully digital accounts and support. Digital-only banks often provide lower fees and higher interest rates on savings because they operate without physical branch expenses. These banks compete with traditional institutions by offering faster services and streamlined user experiences.

However, digital banking introduces challenges. Not all individuals have equal access to technology, creating barriers for those without smartphones, internet access, or digital literacy. Digital banking also increases cybersecurity risks, as online accounts are targets for hackers and scammers. While digital transformation improves efficiency, it also requires customers to be more proactive about protecting their accounts and personal data.

Traditional banks are adapting by modernizing their systems, introducing mobile apps, and integrating digital services. The digital transformation of banking is not a trend—it is the new foundation of how The financial services industry operate.

Cybersecurity in Finance

As finance becomes increasingly digital, cybersecurity has become one of the most critical issues in the industry. Financial institutions handle vast amounts of sensitive information, including account numbers, personal identification, credit histories, and transaction data. This makes them prime targets for cyberattacks. Hackers, fraudsters, and criminal networks constantly attempt to exploit weaknesses in banking systems, payment platforms, and consumer accounts.

Cybersecurity threats include phishing scams, ransomware attacks, identity theft, account hacking, and data breaches. Phishing scams are among the most common threats, involving fake emails or messages designed to trick individuals into sharing passwords or financial information. Ransomware attacks involve hackers locking an institution's systems and demanding payment to restore access. Data breaches can expose customer information, leading to fraud and long-term financial damage.

Financial institutions invest heavily in cybersecurity measures such as encryption, multi-factor authentication, fraud monitoring systems, and secure network infrastructure. Many banks also use AI-powered cybersecurity tools to detect unusual account activity and prevent unauthorized transactions. While these protections are strong, cybercriminals constantly evolve their methods, meaning cybersecurity must be continuously updated and improved.

Individuals also play a major role in financial cybersecurity. Strong passwords, secure online habits, avoiding suspicious links, and monitoring accounts regularly can significantly reduce risk. Consumers must also be cautious with public Wi-Fi networks and ensure their devices are protected with security updates.

Cybersecurity is not just about preventing theft—it is about protecting trust. Financial systems rely on consumer confidence. If customers cannot trust that their money and information are safe, the entire system becomes unstable. In a world where The financial services industry is increasingly digital, cybersecurity is not an optional feature. It is a fundamental requirement for stability and survival.

Technology as the Future of Financial Services

Technology is reshaping finance at every level, from how individuals manage daily spending to how global markets operate. FinTech has expanded access and convenience, blockchain has introduced new systems of trust and decentralization, artificial intelligence has improved efficiency and analytics, digital banking has transformed consumer interactions, and cybersecurity has become essential for protecting modern financial systems.

The role of technology in finance will only continue to grow. Innovations will create new opportunities for faster transactions, improved financial inclusion, and more personalized services. At the same time, these advancements will introduce new risks, requiring stronger regulation, ethical oversight, and consumer education. For individuals, understanding financial technology is no longer optional. It is a critical part of navigating the modern economy with awareness, security, and confidence.

SUSTAINABLE AND ETHICAL INVESTING

Sustainable and ethical investing has become an increasingly important part of modern financial decision-making. As global awareness of environmental issues, social inequality, and corporate responsibility continues to grow, investors are no longer focused solely on financial returns. Many now want their investments to reflect their personal values and contribute positively to society and the environment. This shift has led to the rise of Environmental, Social, and Governance (ESG) investing, impact investing, and ethical screening strategies that aim to balance profit with purpose.

Sustainable investing represents a broader transformation in how financial success is defined. Instead of measuring success only through profit margins or portfolio growth, investors are also considering how companies affect the world around them. This includes evaluating how businesses treat employees, manage environmental resources, and maintain ethical leadership practices. As a result, sustainable investing is reshaping the financial landscape by encouraging companies to operate more responsibly while still delivering competitive returns.

This chapter explores the key principles of ESG investing, the rise of impact investing, the methods used for ethical screening, the financial performance of sustainable investments, and the growing influence of shareholder activism. Together, these concepts illustrate how finance is evolving to reflect both economic goals and social responsibility.

Understanding ESG Principles

Environmental, Social, and Governance (ESG) principles form the foundation of sustainable investing. These three categories provide a framework for evaluating companies beyond traditional financial metrics.

The environmental component focuses on how a company impacts the natural world. This includes carbon emissions, energy efficiency, waste management, water usage, and efforts to reduce environmental harm. Companies that prioritize renewable energy, sustainable production methods, and environmental protection are often viewed more favorably by ESG investors. Environmental responsibility has become especially important as climate change and resource scarcities continue to influence global markets and government policies.

The social component examines how a company treats people. This includes employee relations, workplace safety, diversity and inclusion, community engagement, and customer satisfaction. Companies with strong social practices tend to have better reputations, higher employee retention, and stronger long-term stability. Social responsibility also extends to supply chain ethics, ensuring that products are not made through exploitative labor practices.

Governance refers to how a company is managed and led. Strong governance includes transparent accounting practices, ethical leadership, fair executive compensation, and accountability to shareholders. Companies with poor governance structures are more vulnerable to corruption, fraud, and mismanagement, which can negatively affect investor confidence and long-term performance.

ESG investing involves analyzing these three factors together to assess a company's overall sustainability and ethical standing. Investors increasingly use ESG ratings and data to guide their decisions, recognizing that responsible business practices can contribute to long-term financial resilience.

The Rise of Impact Investing

Impact investing represents an evolution of sustainable investing. While ESG investing focuses on evaluating companies based on sustainability factors, impact investing goes a step further by intentionally seeking investments that generate measurable positive outcomes.

Impact investors aim to create both financial returns and social or environmental benefits. This could include investing in renewable energy projects, affordable housing initiatives, education technology, healthcare access programs, or clean water infrastructure. The key difference is intentionality—impact investments are designed specifically to produce positive change, not just avoid harm.

One of the defining features of impact investing is measurability. Investors often track specific outcomes such as reduced carbon emissions, improved access to education, or increased employment in underserved communities. This allows investors to evaluate whether their capital is making a meaningful difference.

Impact investing has gained popularity among institutional investors, philanthropic organizations, and individuals who want their money to contribute to global challenges. It reflects a growing belief that financial markets can be used as tools for solving social and environmental problems, not just generating profit.

However, impact investing also presents challenges. Measuring impact can be complex, and not all outcomes are easily quantified. There is also a risk of "impact washing," where companies exaggerate their social or environmental contributions. As the field grows, transparency and accountability are becoming increasingly important.

Ethical Screening and Investment Criteria

Ethical screening is a strategy used by investors to include or exclude companies based on moral, social, or environmental standards. This approach allows investors to align their portfolios with their personal values while avoiding industries or practices they consider harmful.

Negative screening involves excluding companies or industries that do not meet ethical standards. Common exclusions include tobacco, weapons manufacturing, fossil fuels, gambling, and industries associated with human rights violations. Investors who use negative screening aim to avoid supporting activities they find socially or environmentally damaging.

Positive screening focuses on selecting companies that demonstrate strong ethical performance. This may include businesses with strong environmental policies, fair labor practices, diverse leadership, or contributions to social good. Instead of avoiding harm, positive screening actively supports companies that promote beneficial outcomes.

Some investors also use norm-based screening, which evaluates companies based on international standards such as human rights agreements, environmental treaties, and labor regulations. Companies that violate these standards may be excluded from investment portfolios.

Ethical screening allows investors to create portfolios that reflect their values, but it also requires careful research. Different investors may have different definitions of what is considered ethical, and there is often no universal standard. As a result, ethical investing involves both financial analysis and personal judgment.

Financial Performance of Sustainable Investments

One of the most common misconceptions about sustainable and ethical investing is that it sacrifices financial returns. In reality, research increasingly shows that ESG-focused investments can perform competitively with traditional investments, and in some cases may outperform them over the long term.

Companies with strong ESG practices often demonstrate better risk management, stronger brand reputation, and greater operational stability. For example, companies that invest in environmental sustainability may reduce long-term costs through energy efficiency. Similarly, companies with strong governance structures are less likely to experience scandals, legal issues, or financial mismanagement.

Sustainable investments also tend to be more resilient during periods of market volatility. Investors who focus on long-term environmental and social trends may benefit from exposure to industries such as renewable energy, clean technology, and sustainable agriculture, which are expected to grow as global priorities shift.

However, performance can vary depending on market conditions and specific investment choices. Not all ESG funds are the same, and some may include companies with only minimal sustainability commitments. This makes careful analysis important when evaluating sustainable investment opportunities.

Overall, evidence suggests that ethical investing does not require sacrificing returns. Instead, it may enhance long-term performance by focusing on companies that are better prepared for future economic, environmental, and regulatory challenges.

The Role of Shareholder Activism

Shareholder activism is a powerful mechanism that allows investors to influence corporate behavior. Instead of simply holding shares passively, activist shareholders use their ownership stakes to advocate for change within companies.

Shareholder activists may push companies to adopt stronger environmental policies, improve labor conditions, increase transparency, or change governance structures. This can be done through shareholder proposals, voting rights, public campaigns, or direct engagement with company leadership.

One of the most significant impacts of shareholder activism is its ability to drive corporate accountability. Companies that face pressure from shareholders are often more likely to improve sustainability practices and address ethical concerns. This creates a feedback loop where investor expectations shape corporate behavior, and corporate behavior influences investor decisions.

Institutional investors, such as pension funds and large asset managers, play a major role in shareholder activism due to their large ownership stakes. However, individual investors can also participate, especially through collective investment platforms or ESG-focused funds that engage in activism on their behalf.

Shareholder activism demonstrates that investors are not passive participants in the financial system. Instead, they can actively shape the direction of corporate behavior and influence broader social and environmental outcomes.

The Future of Sustainable and Ethical Finance

Sustainable and ethical investing represents a significant shift in the financial world. It reflects a growing recognition that financial decisions have real-world consequences beyond profit and loss. As climate change, social inequality, and corporate accountability become more pressing global issues, ESG principles and impact investing are expected to play an even larger role in shaping financial markets.

The future of investing will likely involve greater transparency, improved data on sustainability performance, and increased integration of ethical considerations into mainstream finance. Investors who understand these trends will be better positioned to make informed decisions that align with both financial goals and personal values.

Sustainable investing is not a passing trend—it is a long-term transformation of how finance interacts with society. It demonstrates that profitability and responsibility do not have to be opposing forces, but can instead work together to create a more balanced and resilient financial system.

GLOBAL PERSPECTIVES ON FINANCIAL SERVICES

As we delve into this chapter, we broaden our view to encompass the global landscape of financial services. Explore the interconnectedness of financial markets, regulatory frameworks, and diverse economic systems, providing a comprehensive understanding of the dynamics that shape the world of international finance.

Global Financial Markets

Navigate through the intricacies of global financial markets, understanding how different markets operate and influence each other. Explore the roles of major financial centers, such as Wall Street, London, and Hong Kong, and gain insights into the factors that drive global market trends.

International Banking and Trade Finance

Discover the pivotal role played by international banks in facilitating global trade and finance. From letters of credit to trade financing, understand the mechanisms that support cross-border transactions. Explore how financial institutions navigate the complexities of international regulations and diverse economic conditions.

Currency Markets and Exchange Rates

Dive into the world of currency markets, exploring the factors that influence exchange rates and international trade. Understand the role of central banks in managing currency values and how fluctuations impact businesses and investors across borders.

Global Investment Opportunities and Risks

Explore the array of investment opportunities available on a global scale. From investing in emerging markets to participating in international funds, gain insights into the potential returns and risks associated with diversifying your portfolio across different regions.

Cross-Cultural Financial Management

In a globally connected financial world, understanding cross-cultural financial management is crucial. Explore how cultural nuances impact financial decision-making, negotiation styles, and business practices. Gain insights into effective communication and collaboration in international financial settings.

Emerging Technologies in Global Finance

As we delve deeper into the impact of emerging technologies on the global financial landscape, it is essential to examine how blockchain, artificial intelligence (AI), and financial technology (FinTech) are fundamentally reshaping traditional financial services.

Blockchain technology, known for its decentralized and secure nature, is revolutionizing the way transactions are conducted. Smart contracts, built on blockchain, automate and enhance the efficiency of complex financial agreements, reducing the need for intermediaries. This not only streamlines cross-border transactions but also ensures transparency and trust among involved parties.

Artificial intelligence plays a pivotal role in data analysis, risk assessment, and fraud detection within the financial sector. Machine learning algorithms can process vast amounts of data, providing valuable insights for investment decisions and risk management. Additionally, AI-driven robo-advisors are becoming increasingly popular, offering personalized investment advice and management services to a global audience.

FinTech innovations are fostering financial inclusion and accessibility. Mobile payment systems, peer-to-peer lending platforms, and digital wallets are providing efficient alternatives to traditional banking, especially in regions with limited access to financial services. These technologies are breaking down barriers and enabling individuals worldwide to participate in the global financial ecosystem.

Sustainable Finance and ESG Investing

In response to the growing awareness of environmental, social, and governance (ESG) factors, the financial industry is witnessing a paradigm shift towards sustainable finance. Financial institutions are incorporating ESG criteria into their investment strategies, considering the environmental impact, social responsibility, and corporate governance practices of businesses.

Sustainable finance extends beyond ethical considerations; it also presents attractive investment opportunities. Green bonds, impact investing, and ESG-focused funds are gaining prominence, allowing investors to support environmentally and socially responsible projects while achieving financial returns.

Global Regulatory Frameworks

Navigating the complexities of international financial transactions requires a deep understanding of the regulatory frameworks that govern them. Organizations like the International Monetary Fund (IMF) and the World Bank play crucial roles in establishing and promoting global financial stability through cooperation and policy coordination.

Regulatory compliance is a significant challenge for financial institutions operating across borders. Harmonizing regulations ensures a level playing field and reduces the risk of financial crises. The collaboration between countries and international organizations is essential for creating effective regulatory frameworks that balance innovation with risk mitigation.

Cybersecurity in International Finance

The increasing reliance on digital platforms in international finance has heightened the importance of cybersecurity. Financial institutions face evolving threats from cybercriminals seeking to exploit vulnerabilities in the interconnected global financial infrastructure.

Robust cybersecurity measures are necessary to safeguard sensitive data, protect against financial fraud, and ensure the resilience of digital financial systems. Continuous innovation in cybersecurity technologies, coupled with international collaboration, is essential to stay ahead of emerging threats and maintain the integrity of the global financial ecosystem.

Geopolitical Influences on Financial Markets

Geopolitical events and trends wield substantial influence over the stability and performance of global financial markets. Political decisions, trade agreements, and diplomatic relations create both opportunities and challenges for investors and financial institutions operating on the international stage.

Trade tensions, sanctions, and geopolitical conflicts can lead to market volatility and impact investment strategies. Understanding the geopolitical landscape is crucial for making informed financial decisions, as geopolitical developments can shape economic policies, influence currency values, and affect the profitability of international investments.

The Future of Global Finance

Looking ahead, the future of global finance holds exciting possibilities and potential disruptions. The rise of digital currencies, including central bank digital currencies (CBDCs) and Cryptocurrencies, may reshape the traditional banking system and redefine how financial transactions are conducted on a global scale.

Changes in global economic power dynamics, driven by factors such as technological advancements and geopolitical shifts, will impact investment opportunities and strategic decision-making. International cooperation will play a pivotal role in addressing challenges and fostering a resilient global financial ecosystem that adapts to evolving trends.

In this dynamic environment, businesses and investors must remain agile, embracing innovation and staying informed about emerging trends to thrive in the ever-evolving world of international finance.

THE IMPORTANCE OF CONTINUOUS LEARNING IN MASTERING FINANCIAL SERVICES

The financial services industry is not a static field. It is constantly shaped by new regulations, evolving markets, technological breakthroughs, and changing consumer behavior. What is considered best practice today may be outdated within a few years—or even months. Because of this constant change, continuous learning is not optional for anyone working in or engaging with financial services. It is a core requirement for long-term success, adaptability, and informed decision-making.

Mastering The financial services industry is not a destination but an ongoing process. Even experienced professionals regularly update their knowledge to stay relevant in an industry that never stands still. Investors, advisors, entrepreneurs, and consumers alike benefit from maintaining a mindset of lifelong learning. This chapter highlights why continuous education matters, how it can be pursued effectively, and how it strengthens both professional capability and personal financial confidence.

Lifelong Learning in Finance

Lifelong learning refers to the ongoing process of developing knowledge and skills throughout one's life. In financial services, this mindset is especially important because financial systems are deeply connected to global economic conditions, technological change, and government policy. These forces are always shifting, which means financial understanding must also evolve.

Markets do not behave in predictable ways over long periods. Economic cycles of growth and recession influence investment performance, interest rates, and employment levels. A strategy that works well in one market environment may perform poorly in another. Lifelong learning helps individuals recognize these shifts and adjust their strategies accordingly.

Financial regulations also change regularly in response to economic events, political decisions, and consumer protection needs. New laws may affect taxation, banking practices, lending rules, or investment requirements. Without ongoing learning, individuals risk making outdated financial decisions that could lead to inefficiency or even legal issues.

Technology adds another layer of change. Digital banking, FinTech platforms, artificial intelligence, and blockchain systems continue to reshape how The financial services industry operate. Staying informed about these developments ensures that individuals and professionals can take advantage of new tools while also understanding the risks they may introduce.

A lifelong learning mindset encourages curiosity, adaptability, and resilience. It shifts financial thinking from fixed knowledge to continuous improvement. This approach helps individuals remain confident in uncertain environments and better prepared for financial challenges.

Professional Development Opportunities

There are many ways to develop financial knowledge and skills throughout a career or personal learning journey. Professional development in The financial services industry is not limited to formal education—it includes a wide range of learning experiences that build expertise over time.

Formal education, such as university degrees in finance, economics, or business administration, provides a strong foundation. However, financial learning does not stop at graduation. Many professionals pursue advanced certifications such as Chartered Financial Analyst (CFA), Certified Financial Planner (CFP), or accounting designations to deepen their expertise and credibility. These qualifications often open doors to higher-level roles and specialized career paths.

Workshops, seminars, and industry conferences also play an important role in professional development. These events allow individuals to learn directly from experts, explore current industry trends, and engage in discussions about emerging challenges. Conferences often highlight real-world case studies, giving participants insight into how financial theories are applied in practice.

On-the-job learning is another valuable form of development. Working in The financial services industry exposes individuals to real-world decision-making, problem-solving, and client interaction. Over time, practical experience becomes one of the most powerful learning tools, especially when combined with reflection and mentorship.

Self-directed learning is also increasingly important. Reading financial publications, studying market reports, and following economic news help individuals stay informed about global financial developments. Those who actively seek knowledge outside formal environments often develop stronger analytical and decision-making skills.

Continuous professional development strengthens not only technical knowledge but also critical thinking, adaptability, and confidence in navigating complex financial situations.

Staying Informed about Regulatory Changes

Regulation is one of the most important and fast-changing aspects of financial services. Governments and regulatory bodies continuously update laws to address new risks, technological developments, and economic conditions. These changes can affect everything from investment rules and tax policies to banking procedures and consumer protections.

Staying informed about regulatory changes is essential for maintaining compliance and avoiding financial or legal consequences. For professionals, failing to understand updated regulations can lead to serious penalties or reputational damage. For individuals, it can result in missed opportunities or unintended financial errors.

One effective way to stay informed is by following official regulatory publications and updates from financial authorities. These sources provide direct information about changes in laws and compliance requirements. Financial news outlets and industry reports also help interpret regulatory updates and explain their practical implications.

Many financial organizations provide internal training and compliance programs to ensure that employees understand new regulations. These programs are especially important in banks, investment firms, and insurance companies, where compliance standards are strict and constantly evolving.

Understanding regulatory changes also requires interpreting how they affect financial strategies. For example, changes in tax law may influence investment decisions, while new lending regulations may impact borrowing opportunities. Staying informed allows individuals and professionals to adapt quickly and maintain effective financial planning.

Harnessing Technology for Learning

Technology has transformed how people access financial education. Learning is no longer limited to classrooms or printed textbooks. Digital platforms now provide instant access to a wide range of financial knowledge, making continuous education more accessible than ever before.

Online courses allow individuals to study financial topics at their own pace. These courses often cover subjects such as investment strategies, financial analysis, accounting principles, and risk management. Many are designed by universities or professional organizations, ensuring high-quality content.

Webinars and virtual seminars provide real-time learning opportunities with experts from the financial industry. These sessions often include interactive discussions, allowing participants to ask questions and engage directly with instructors.

Mobile apps and digital tools also support financial learning. Some platforms offer simulated investing environments, allowing users to practice trading and portfolio management without real financial risk. Others provide budgeting tools that help individuals understand personal finance in a practical way.

Artificial intelligence is also playing a growing role in education. AI-powered learning systems can personalize content based on user progress, strengths, and weaknesses. This makes learning more efficient and tailored to individual needs.

Technology not only improves access to education but also encourages continuous engagement. Financial learning becomes more flexible, interactive, and integrated into daily life.

Building a Professional Network

Networking is a crucial component of continuous learning in financial services. Building relationships with others in the industry provides opportunities to exchange knowledge, gain new perspectives, and stay informed about industry developments.

A strong professional network includes peers, mentors, colleagues, and industry experts. Each connection offers different insights and experiences that contribute to overall understanding. Mentors, in particular, can provide guidance based on real-world experience, helping individuals navigate complex financial decisions or career challenges.

Professional organizations and associations also provide valuable networking opportunities. These groups often host events, workshops, and forums where members can connect and share ideas. Being part of a professional community helps individuals stay engaged with industry trends and build long-term relationships.

Networking is not only about career advancement. It is also about learning from others' experiences. The financial services industry is a broad field, and no single individual can master every area alone. Collaboration and shared knowledge strengthen overall understanding and create opportunities for innovation.

Digital networking platforms have also expanded opportunities for connection. Online professional communities allow individuals to engage with global financial experts, participate in discussions, and access a wide range of perspectives.

Continuous Learning as a Financial Mindset

Continuous learning is more than an activity—it is a mindset that shapes how individuals approach financial services. It encourages curiosity, adaptability, and openness to change. In a field where uncertainty is constant, this mindset becomes a major advantage.

Financial mastery is not achieved through a single course, book, or experience. It is developed over time through consistent effort, reflection, and adaptation. Those who commit to learning throughout their lives are better prepared to navigate market changes, regulatory updates, and technological advancements.

This mindset also supports better decision-making. Individuals who continuously learn are more likely to understand risks, recognize opportunities, and avoid common financial mistakes. They are better equipped to adjust strategies when conditions change, rather than relying on outdated assumptions.

A Lifelong Commitment to Financial Growth

The financial world will continue to evolve. New technologies will emerge, markets will shift, and global economic conditions will change. In this environment, continuous learning is the foundation of long-term success.

Mastering The financial services industry is not about reaching a final level of knowledge. It is about maintaining the ability to grow, adapt, and respond to new information. Whether through formal education, professional experience, technology-driven learning, or networking, every effort contributes to stronger financial understanding.

By embracing continuous learning, individuals position themselves not only for professional advancement but also for greater financial confidence and resilience. In a world defined by constant change, the ability to keep learning is one of the most valuable financial skills of all.

---

[i] Primerica is a registered trademark of its owner. This book is not affiliated with, endorsed by, or sponsored by Primerica.

www.ingramcontent.com/pod-product-compliance
Lightning Source LLC
LaVergne TN
LVHW022204200926
848481LV00006B/1843